THE SCRAMBLER'S DOZEN

THE SCRAMBLER'S DOZEN

The 12 Shots Every Golfer Needs to Score Like the Pros

Mike McGetrick
with Tom Ferrell

A Mountain Lion Book

HarperResource
An Imprint of HarperCollins*Publishers*

HarperCollins books may be purchased for educational, business, or sales promotional use. For information, please write to: Special Markets Department, HarperCollins Publishers Inc., 10 East 53rd Street, New York, New York 10022.

FIRST EDITION
Designed by Joseph Rutt

Printed on acid-free paper.

Library of Congress Cataloging-in-Publication Data
McGetrick, Mike, 1959–
The scrambler's dozen: the 12 shots every golfer needs to score like the pros/Mike McGetrick with Tom Ferrell—1st ed.
p.   cm.
ISBN 0-06-270246-7
1. Swing (Golf) I. Ferrell, Tom; 1962–   II. Title
GV979.S9 M28 2000
796.352'3—dc21

00 01 02 03 04 ❖/RRD 10 9 8 7 6 5 4 3 2 1

*For my parents, Mack and Sandra McGetrick,
and my in-laws, Les and Jackie Timms,
for all of their love and support.*

Contents

Foreword

The thing about golf is that you can never quite get a handle on it. Just when you think you've got the game figured out, you find yourself in a new situation and have to reach into your shotmaking bag of tricks. That's what keeps golf interesting and fun, whether you're a Tour professional or a weekend player. Mike McGetrick has worked with golfers of every level, and he knows all about shotmaking. With Mike's help, I've just finished the best year of my career, winning two major championships and earning a spot in the LPGA Hall of Fame. But it wasn't because my game was perfect. It was because I was more comfortable than ever before at hitting the shot that the moment required. I'll give you an example. At the 1999 U.S. Women's Open at Old Waverly Golf Club, I was on the seventh hole of the final round. I had a two-shot lead at the time, not much when you consider the caliber of the other golfers in contention. At the seventh, I hit my ball into a bunker, and it ended up in a buried lie. Rather than letting myself get uptight about my bad luck, I simply remembered my shotmaking fundamentals and played the shot. Fortunately, I was able to get the ball close, sink the putt for par and go on to win the championship. This book can help you develop that same kind of confidence. Mike shows you basic shotmaking techniques and then teaches you how to use those fundamentals to be able to execute a strategic shot in almost any situation the golf course can present. Mike also gives you some rules for practicing these shots so that you'll be prepared when you need to hit them on the course. Believe me, this game is tough. Working with Mike has helped me find new ways to save strokes in almost every round. It will help you, too. Enjoy *The Scrambler's Dozen.* I think you'll find Mike to be as good a coach and friend to you as he is to me.

—Juli Inkster,
1999 U.S. Women's Open and
LPGA Championship winner

Acknowledgments

Until undertaking this project, I had no idea how much work went into producing a book. I can honestly tell you it wouldn't have been possible without the help of my fellow teaching professional Lana Ortega, who not only helped edit the book, but also provided invaluable feedback on the techniques and shots included; Tom Ferrell, my longtime writing partner; PGA professionals Don Hurter and Dave Collins, who made me defend every piece on instruction that went into this project; Randy Voorhees from Mountain Lion, a great agent and supporter; and Bill Swartz and Dom Lupo for their wonderful artwork.

Introduction

Congratulations. By picking up this book, you've made a commitment to your golf game. And commitment is what it takes to improve your scoring. Golf is a simple game in theory, but as you know, the skills and techniques required to excel are very complex. Whether you're playing for a national championship, a club championship or simply trying to beat your personal best, you have to develop trust in your swing, your short game and your strategies. Tour players must trust their decisions and their ability to execute shots on the golf course in order to win tournaments and make a living. You have to do the same thing to get the greatest rewards from your golf experiences. In this book, I'll show you how, using the same methods I use when I coach some of the best players in the world.

Golf's most unique element is that no two rounds and no two courses are ever the same. Weather conditions change. So do ground conditions. Golf courses occupy flat sites and traverse hilly territory. A change as simple as the position of a pin can completely alter your shotmaking options. So golf is about adaptability, recognizing how conditions and circumstances will affect your shots and altering your strategy and execution to fit the specific requirements of the shot.

We marvel at the scores the Tour professionals shoot, and it's true that most of us will never know what it feels like to fire a 65 on Sunday with the tournament on the line. Top professionals do it by squeezing every ounce out of their games. Like you, they don't hit the ball perfectly every time. They miss fairways and greens. They struggle in difficult conditions. But they also know what it takes to fade the ball around a tree or to hit a soft flop shot to a tough pin. When they find themselves in the fairway with 100 yards to the target, they know how to play a number of different shots depending on conditions. They understand when and how to chip or pitch or putt from off the green. And they know how to practice so that they are rarely in unfamiliar situations on the golf course. In other words, they give themselves scoring chances even when things are not going perfectly.

Anyone can play good golf on those magical days when every shot is pure and every putt is dropping. The key is to develop that sixth sense for scoring—knowing how to get the ball into the hole from anywhere. That's what I want to show you in this book. Scrambling isn't reserved only for your off-days. Good golfers scramble in every round. Good scramblers are always good scorers.

When I sat down to develop this book, I spent many hours determining which shots to include. The twelve shots I chose to feature are excellent additions to your golf game in and of themselves. But each of them is truly a jumping-off point that will allow you to develop not just a dozen new weapons but many, many more. Shotmaking is much more than simply curving the ball or hitting it low and high. It's understanding how the lie, the wind, the contour of the target and the hazards of the course will affect your decision-making process. As you develop a feel for these subtle differences, you will find yourself instinctively modifying the twelve featured shots to fit very specific needs. That's when you're really playing golf.

And now, play away.

THE SCRAMBLER'S DOZEN

THE FADE

Working the Ball Right and Left

"You can talk to a fade, but a hook won't listen."
—Lee Trevino

You've been playing golf long enough to know that, on the course at least, the shortest path between two points is rarely a straight line. To improve your scoring, you have to master the basic elements of shot-making—working the ball from left to right and from right to left. The golf course never lets you rest. There are dogleg holes to contend with, tucked pins, wind conditions, trees and other obstacles. The player who has an idea how to affect the movement of the golf ball has a distinct advantage over the player who just hits and hopes.

In this chapter, we'll cover two of the basic shotmaking elements—the left-to-right fade and the right-to-left draw. Whether you are a beginner, a scratch player or even a professional, you need to practice continuously to improve your shotmaking skills. As your shotmaking improves, you'll find that not only are you playing better golf, you're having more fun.

FEATURED SHOT: THE FADE

Most weekend golfers live in fear of the slice. To them, a fade is often guilty by association. You should not undervalue the fade as a shot-making choice, however, no matter what your skill level. Many of the game's greatest players built their games around a fade. Recreational golfers often complain about a lack of consistency in their games. The fade is probably the most consistent shot they could develop. The elements that produce a fade already exist in their swings, they simply aren't tamed enough to soften the left-to-right movement of the ball so as to make it predictable and useful.

Even if a fade costs you a couple of yards off the tee, it will deliver greater accuracy and, for most golfers, find more fairways. On approaches to the green, a fade will fly high and land softly, just the characteristics you're looking for in an iron shot. When executed properly, the fade is one of the most controlled shots in golf and should be the first step you take in building your shotmaking repertoire.

Visualizing the Fade

All great shotmakers have great "eyes," and not only in their heads. These players also have mastered the art of seeing with their mind's eye. One of the most important things you can add to your preshot routine is visualization. Stand behind the ball and imagine the shot coming off just as you planned it, starting slightly left of the target and gradually bending back to the right. This visualization establishes a goal that your mind will work to achieve. In other words, with proper visualization you begin to move toward execution rather than simply swinging and hoping.

Setting Up for the Fade

The first adjustments you need to make to produce a left-to-right fade come during the setup. By adjusting your setup, you can influence the path of your swing and the angle of the clubface at impact—the two principal factors in curving the golf ball.

Start with club selection. A faded shot will fly slightly shorter and run less than a straight shot, so start your preparation by taking one or even two clubs more than usual, depending on the amount of curve you are playing. You must also remember that less-lofted clubs will tend to produce more left-to-right movement on the ball than shorter clubs with more loft. So if you really need to bend the shot, you should consider a longer, less-lofted club.

Proper alignment is crucial to producing a shot that performs as you have visualized it. For the basic fade, start by aligning your clubface at the target, just as you would for a straight shot. Your body alignment and the path of your swing will apply the proper spin to make the ball curve.

In this basic fade technique, the degree to which you open your body at address dictates the amount of curve you will get on the shot. Many high-handicappers make the mistake of fighting left-to-right ball movement by opening up even more so they're aiming farther left. This will only cause more left-to-right movement, since the club will cut across the ball at a greater angle, imparting more sidespin.

Align your feet, knees, hips, shoulders, arms and eyes down the line on which you want the ball to start. Play the ball about two inches forward of where you normally play it in your stance. This ball position complements an open body position and encourages a higher trajec-

tory. Before gripping the club, make sure the clubface is still aligned at the target. Now, use a slightly tighter than normal grip pressure in both hands for the fade. A tighter grip pressure will help you delay the release of your hands so they don't close the clubface prior to impact.

Now just make a regular golf swing, swinging the club back along the line of your shoulders. The adjustments you have made to your setup and alignment will cause the clubhead to swing slightly across the target line on the backswing and then "cut" the ball through the hitting area.

Focus on your rhythm, particularly the transition between your

A good fade setup has the clubface aimed at the target, with the body aligned to the left in order to create the left-to-right shape of the shot.

backswing and forward swing. The most common flaw that will turn a fade into a slice is starting the downswing too quickly with the upper body. Instead, concentrate on fully completing the backswing and starting down gradually, allowing your arms, hands and clubhead to accelerate into the impact area. Rotate your upper body to the left as you swing into your finish, being sure to fully complete the shot.

Remember, the key to the fade is to start the ball to the left and work it back the same distance to the right. If you can do that, you'll have a powerful tool in your shotmaking bag.

Advanced Fade Techniques

The alignment-based fade technique we've discussed in the past few pages will definitely teach you to hit a left-to-right shot. But I've found that the majority of my Tour students have developed their own subtle ways of creating a fade. You may find some of these methods useful in certain situations.

The Outside-In Swing Path   To hit what I call the path fade, align the clubface not to the end target but along the line on which you want the ball to start. Now open your body correspondingly. Still using the setup adjustments we discussed in the previous section, make an exaggerated out-to-in swing, swinging the club back outside the shoulder line. You may feel like you're lifting the club with your arms and your hands, reducing the amount of body turn. That's okay. As you swing through the ball, make a conscious effort to cut the shot, swinging across the original target line. Maintain a firm grip pressure to prevent your hands from fully releasing. The direction of your swing path as you approach impact will control the amount of fade on the ball.

The Reverse Release   If you're like most golfers, you strive for a full and fast release in order to get maximum distance. To hit a fade, however, you want to limit the release of the hands. By increasing your grip pressure at address, you have taken a big step toward delaying

To create a path fade, swing the golf club to the outside of the target line on the way back.

Another way of fading the ball is the reverse release, characterized by the "chicken-wing" position of the left arm.

your release at impact, but now, as you swing through the shot, I want you to get the feeling of leading with your hands and resisting the release. You should feel that your hands are leading the club head into the hitting area. Keep them ahead of the clubhead as long as possible. Rather than allowing the right hand to take over, think of a finish in which the clubhead is above your head, with the left arm slightly bent in a "chicken-wing" position.

The Weak Grip Some players have very sensitive hands and have the ability to alter their shot shapes by making slight adjustments to their grips. You may want to try weakening your left-hand grip, gradually turning it to the left until you see one or no knuckles at address. A weakened grip will cause you to swing the club more with your hands and arms and will also inhibit the release—perfect launch conditions for a fade.

Experiment with these methods of hitting the fade. As you do, make mental notes of what kinds of trajectories and shapes these various adjustments produce. You may find that a combination of setup, path and release modifications work best for you. Be sure to integrate faded shots into your practice routine. That's how you develop the feel that good shotmakers are known for.

GREAT FADERS

If you think that playing a fade is really just giving in to your slice, consider that some of the best players the game has ever seen faded the ball consistently. That's because a repeatable fade keeps the ball on target and in play.

Lee Trevino Though Lee Trevino is one of the greatest ball-strikers in golf history, his bread-and-butter shot was the low fade. Learning the game on the windswept plains of Texas, he knew that keeping the ball low to the ground and being able to predict its movement in flight would let him play with confidence. That confidence allowed him to become one of the top players of his generation and to remain on top throughout his career.

Jack Nicklaus Nicklaus redefined the way the game was played when he emerged from an outstanding amateur career in 1962. With power to spare, Nicklaus focused on strategy and control. By developing a high fade, particularly with his long irons, he was able to go after pins that no one else could touch—without taking big gambles.

Ben Hogan Plagued by an uncontrollable hook early in his career, Hogan poured his legendary work ethic into producing a hook-proof swing. His success spawned hundreds of analyses and articles about "Hogan's secret." After making the transition to the fade, Hogan won nine major championships and etched his mark on golf.

Fred Couples When you watch Fred Couples swing the golf club, what strikes you is the easy tempo he is able to achieve. He minimizes his body motion and lets his hands and his great timing do a lot of the work. In order for this to happen, he sets up in an open position and makes a classic fade swing. Looking at the consistency and longevity he's achieved in his career, it's hard to argue with his method.

ON THE COURSE

Living with a Slice

Unless you're an advanced golfer, there will be days when your slice just won't come under control. While you should continue to work on the fundamentals of producing a more moderate and controlled fade, there are some things you can do during a less than perfect ball-striking round to incorporate the ball's movement into your game.

1. Align yourself to the left of the target to allow for the left-to-right flight of the ball. Visualize both the starting and finishing position of the ball. Remember that the longer, less-lofted clubs will impart more sidespin for more left-to-right movement, so adjust your alignment accordingly.

2. Use the entire tee box. If you tee up on the far right side of the tee box, you'll open up more of the left side of the fairway, allowing more room for your natural shot shape.

3. Consider a set of offset clubs. Offset clubs, where the clubhead is positioned slightly behind the shaft, help keep your hands in front of the ball and give the clubface more time to square up before impact.

4. Play a two-piece ball. A two-piece ball that produces less backspin will also produce less sidespin.

THE DRAW

If you polled average golfers and asked them to pick the shot they'd most like to hit consistently, the draw would be an overwhelming winner. Golfers see the draw as the mark of a good player, and with good reason. In order to produce a reliable draw that starts to the right of the target and gently curves back, you have to have good fundamentals and excellent tempo, rhythm and timing.

The mistake I see most golfers make when they try to hit a draw is overexaggerating the role of the hands in the release. They end up releasing the club too early and hitting either a smother-hook or a dead-left pull. In reality, with a few simple setup and swing adjustments, anyone can hit a draw.

The first modification you need to make is with your club selection. A draw produces right-to-left overspin. Generally, a right-to-left shot

To draw the ball, aim the clubface at the target and position the body on a line to the right of the target.

The proper backswing path for the draw is to the inside of the target line.

will fly lower and roll more than a left-to-right shot, so I recommend dropping down a club. In other words, if your standard 150-yard club is a 7-iron, but you plan to hit a draw to the target, go to an 8-iron.

Now you'll need to align yourself properly to encourage a right-to-left movement of the ball. With the clubface aimed at the target or even closed slightly so that it points just left of the target, align your body to the right, along the line you want the ball to start on.

Play the ball back one or two inches from your normal ball position. Lighten your grip pressure slightly in both hands to encourage a good release through the hitting area. A slightly stronger grip will also help you draw the ball. To achieve a stronger grip, rotate your hands to the right until the you can see two or three knuckles on your left hand at address and the V between your thumb and index finger on your right hand points to the outside of your right shoulder.

The most helpful swing key for hitting a draw is to stay relaxed. Take

The follow-through of a draw swing has right arm rotated over left and a low finish.

a few waggles before the swing. Waggle the club back far enough so that you can begin to feel the swing path. Tension in your hands and arms will restrict the proper movement of the body and the clubhead and will prohibit a good release. Swing through the shot toward the point where you want the ball to start. By approaching impact from an inside path, you'll help the clubface naturally close as you release through the ball to produce the draw spin. Concentrate on making a good, fast release, with a low follow-through. If you work on these fundamentals, I think you'll find that the draw is easier to hit than you ever imagined.

JULI INKSTER TAKES CONTROL

LPGA Hall of Fame member and 1999 U.S. Women's Open champion Juli Inkster recently came to me and said she wanted to convert her standard shot from a fade to a draw. I reminded her that she had had great success throughout her career using the fade as her bread-and-butter shot. But she felt that her swing had gotten away from her and that she was losing power—and strokes—by being limited to a left-to-right shot. Over the course of the next season, Juli and I worked on the mechanics of the draw, and gradually her game began to change. She is now in the middle of the most prosperous stretch of an already great career. By drawing the ball, she has gained distance off the tee and confidence in her swing. Rather than feeling that she is hemmed in by her swing and shot type, she has taken control. The confidence you gain is one of the unseen benefits of honing your shotmaking skills. When you know you can make the ball do what you want it to do, you're poised for success.

Chapter Summary

THE FADE

Setup

- Club up one or two clubs (e.g., the distance calls for a 6-iron, but use a 5- or 4-iron when fading the ball)

- Open the clubface first, then grip the golf club

- Aim clubface at the end target

- Align body where you want the ball to start (to the left)

- Position ball two inches forward

- Tighter grip pressure in both hands

Swing

- Swing along the line of your shoulders in the backswing and forward swing

- Focus on a smooth transition to start the forward swing

- Maintain a firm grip pressure throughout the swing

Advanced Techniques

- Outside-in swing path

- Reverse release

- Weak grip

Strategy

- This shot will fly higher and roll less than normal

- Less-lofted clubs produce more sidespin than more lofted ones

- The amount you open your clubface and body determines the amount of curvature

- Setup and swing increases the effective loft of the club you're using

- Know the trajectory and amount of curve for different clubs

- Know how the fade affects distance control

Swing Thoughts

- Visualize the left-to-right ball flight

- "Hang on"—keep hands and wrists firm through the shot

THE DRAW

Setup

- Drop down one or two clubs (e.g., the distance calls for a 6-iron, but use a 8- or 7-iron when drawing the ball)

- Close the clubface first, then grip the golf club

- Aim clubface at the end target

- Align body in direction you want the ball to start (to the right)

- Position ball two inches back

- Lighter grip pressure in both hands

Swing

- Swing along the line of your shoulders on the backswing and forward swing

- Release hands and forearms fully through the hitting area

- Low finish

Strategy

- This shot will fly lower and roll more than normal

- The setup and swing reduces the effective loft of the club you're using

- The amount you close your clubface and body determines the amount of curvature

- Know the trajectory and amount of curve for different clubs

- Know how the draw affects distance control

Swing Thoughts

- Visualize the right-to-left ball flight

- Stay loose—allow the toe of the club to pass the heel through the hitting area to close the clubface

- Low finish

A FEW WORDS ABOUT PRACTICE

Golf is not a game you can easily master. And though the shots you'll find in this book are simple enough that anyone can use them, you will be much better off if you practice to develop consistency. Consistency isn't always about avoiding scrambling. Preparing for your difficult situations is one of the most vital keys to good golf.

At the end of each chapter, you'll find a short section on practicing the shots discussed in that chapter. I recommend that you integrate these drills and games into your practice routine. Not only will practicing these shots help you become a better player, it will make your range time more fun.

There are two basic types of practice—fundamental and competitive. In fundamental practice, you work on the technique required to successfully make a shot. Competitive practice introduces game-day simulation so that you get the feeling of making the shot when there's something riding on the outcome.

Most of the competitive practice you'll read in these pages focuses on the five-ball drill. The five-ball drill is simple. You have five tries at the shot. Using your own standard of an acceptable result, try to make three of five shots acceptable. Give yourself three chances (three sets of five shots) to achieve the goal. If you achieve it before the third set, you're done. But next time, up the ante by making it your goal to hit four acceptable shots out of five. I think you'll agree that competitive practice produces results. Good luck!

Practice Strategies

WORKING THE BALL

Being able to curve the ball from left-to-right and from right-to-left demonstrates your ability to control your body and the clubface at impact. Practice the following drills to help you master the fundamentals of shotmaking: curving the golf ball.

Fundamental Drill

Set up a workstation on the range to practice imparting fade and draw spin on the golf ball. Lay one club down parallel to the target line. Lay another club down to indicate the starting direction of the ball (to the left for a fade, to the right for a draw). Using a 5-iron, aim the clubface so the leading edge is perpendicular to the target line, and align your entire body along the club that indicates the starting direction. Hit curving shots, imagining the shape and trajectory as you hit each shot. Take note of the starting direction of each shot and where the ball ends up relative to your end target. Notice how much carry and roll is produced with each shot when you fade and draw the ball. Also notice the trajectory produced with each shot—this is especially important if you need to curve the ball out of trouble and back into play. Then experiment at working the ball by changing 1) the amount you open and close your clubface and your body alignments, and 2) strengthening and weakening your grip. Your goal is to discover the setup and swing adjustments that make it the easiest for you to hit fades and draws while controlling distance and maintaining accuracy.

Competitive Drill

You can chart your progress at executing fades and draws on the range by using the five-ball drill. You'll use your odd clubs for this drill during one practice session, and your even clubs the next session— that way you will be using all your clubs and balancing out your practice between short irons, mid-irons, long irons and woods. Start by choosing a target on the range. If you start with your odd clubs, you'll hit your SW, 9-iron, 7-iron, 5-iron, 3-iron, 3-wood and driver. Your goal is to hit three of five what you would consider acceptable fades or draws with each club to your target, and you're allowed three attempts before you move on to the next club. Acceptable will, of course, be different for different players, but your score should take into consideration how effectively you 1) impart the desired spin and, 2) control distance and accuracy.

THE BUMP-AND-RUN

Friends in Low—and High—Places

"Hit it Low, Collect the Dough."
—Golfer's proverb

Just as you need to know how to work the ball in both directions in order to get the most out of your game, you also need to know how to control the trajectory of your shots. Most beginners make the mistake of believing that higher shots are better shots. It's fun to hit those long, towering shots, and high shots can be very useful, as I'll show you later in this chapter. But what many golfers don't realize is the value of hitting the ball low. In Hawaii, where the trade winds blow every day, golfers say, "Hit it low, collect the dough." Wind, of course, was a central element of early golf in Scotland and remains so today.

Tiger Woods spent most of 1998 working to develop a swing that would produce a lower, more consistent trajectory with his irons. The results have been startling. With his newfound control, he rarely has the lapses in short-iron play that marked his early career. Tom Watson learned to shape the trajectory of his shots by playing year-round golf in often-windy Kansas City, Missouri. He went on to use his bump-and-run skills to win five British Open titles.

The bump-and-run is golf's original specialty shot, and today it is still one of the most valuable shots you can have in your bag. Knowing how to control the trajectory of your shots gives you a great advantage and helps you adapt your game to different courses and conditions. Adaptability helps you develop a game that travels well and is not dependent on course familiarity. And that is a game that will stand up under pressure.

FEATURED SHOT: THE BUMP-AND-RUN

Golf grew from the Scottish links—treeless, seaside courses that feature numerous dunes, swales and undulations. And, of course, coastal winds. The imperfections of the terrain combined with the unpredictability of the breeze made it very difficult to play high approaches into the green. Instead, the early Scottish players perfected a shot known as the bump-and-run.

I consider a bump-and-run to be any low shot in which the ball flies only part of the way to the target and then runs along the ground the rest of the way. This can be very useful if you have a shot into a green that has a wide opening in front, a green that is elevated or that slopes from back to front with a center or rear pin position.

You can play the bump-and-run with almost any club in your bag. The key to club selection is having a good feel for the carry-to-roll ratio you'll

get from each club. In general, you want to play the bump-and-run using a club with as little loft as possible. This shot is designed to do most of its work on the ground.

After you've selected your club, grip down two or three inches to create a shorter lever that is easier to control, since this is just a partial swing. Stand two or three inches closer to the ball. This will set the shaft in a more vertical position and will encourage a swing that works more down into the ball at impact.

Play the ball back in your stance, about an inch right of center. Not only will this ball position help make sure that you strike the ball first on the forward swing, it will also move your hands ahead of the

To bump the ball low to the ground, you need to play the ball back in your stance, with your hands set slightly ahead.

On the backswing, the clubhead swings to about waist high.

The low clubhead position at the finish is crucial to the bump-and-run, but notice how the body rotates through to face the target.

ball, de-lofting the club slightly. Distribute your weight evenly between the left and right feet, with your upper body set directly on top of your lower body so that your shoulders feel almost parallel to the ground.

The bump-and-run swing is a one-lever motion with minimal wrist hinge. Swing back with very little upper-body rotation. The backswing for this shot is longer than the follow-through. Depending on the distance of the shot, your backswing will be from waist high to shoulder high. Make a smooth transition into the forward swing, leading with your hands, and hit down into the ball. The follow-through is very abbreviated to help keep the ball down, although you should allow your body to rotate through the shot so that you end up facing the target with the golf club in front of you, no higher than waist high. Different clubs will produce different types of shots—pay attention to the carry-and-roll you get as you work on this shot with the various clubs in your bag.

With links-style golf courses cropping up all over the United States, the bump-and-run will be a valuable tool to have in your shotmaking repertoire.

The Knockdown Iron Shot

Low shots are useful from full-shot distances as well, and the knockdown approach is one of the most useful you can learn. Not only will the knockdown shot help you get out of trouble by punching under limbs and branches, but you can use it in all types of wind conditions and allow it to be the basis of any number of creative shots on the course.

To craft a knockdown, you're simply going to extend the bump-and-run's swing technique and allow for a little hand action on the backswing to increase distance. Remember, less is more when it comes to loft. The knockdown swing is a partial swing, so you'll want to use

For a knockdown, play the ball in the center of your stance, with your hands ahead of the ball.

To keep the ball down, the backswing should be three-quarters with limited upper-body rotation and minimal wrist break.

more club than you normally would for the same distance. In other words, if your standard 150-yard club is a 7-iron, but you are playing a knockdown shot, drop down to a 6-iron or even a 5-iron.

Grip down one or two inches on the handle of the golf club. The knockdown is a control shot, so you want to shorten the lever you're swinging. Stand an inch or two closer to the ball to compensate for the shorter lever. Grip the club with a firm grip pressure in both hands. Overactive hands at impact will cause inconsistency with direction.

As you address the ball, stand tall, with your upper body directly on top of your lower body and your shoulders almost level, and move the ball back to the center of your stance to ensure that you'll strike the ball first as you swing through. Set your hands slightly ahead of the ball. A forward hand position will naturally de-loft the clubface, again helping to start the ball on a low trajectory.

The distance of the shot determines the length of the backswing. Concentrate on making a smooth, rhythmic swing with an even transition between the backswing and the forward swing. Stay level through the hitting area, maintaining the tall position you established at address.

You want to lead with your hands on this shot. Focus on returning your hands and the shaft of the club to the same position they were in at address—ahead of the ball. Resist the release. The best tip I can give you for this shot is: A low shot means a low finish. The lower you want to hit it, the more you need to resist the release. Rotate fully with your body on the forward swing so the

Finish the knockdown shot standing tall, with your body rotated toward the target and the clubhead about waist high.

hands can stay ahead of the clubhead. Finish with the golf club in a low position but with your belt buckle facing the target.

THE HIGH SHOT

No matter where you play golf, you will surely encounter times when you need to hit the ball high. A high shot can help you get to a difficult pin position or clear bothersome trees. Now that you are familiar with how to hit curving shots and low shots, it's not much of a stretch to learn how to hit one that rises quickly and flies high.

Depending on how high you plan to hit the ball, you'll need at least one extra club, possibly two. Play the ball about an inch forward of your normal ball position. The key to hitting the ball high is staying behind it from start to finish. Increase your spine tilt by lowering your right shoulder at address. Increasing the spine tilt will position more

For a high shot, move the ball up in your stance, drop the right shoulder and set your hands even with the ball.

This reverse-C finish position results from hanging back on the right side during the forward swing.

weight on your right side and will also open the clubface slightly, helping you add loft. Remember, a high shot requires a high finish.

Make a long, smooth swing, concentrating on a full shoulder and body turn. As you begin the forward swing, make a conscious effort to stay behind the ball and swing along the shoulder tilt you established at address. It should feel as though your weight is lagging back on the right side. Let your hands release fully through the impact area, and swing into a high finish.

FIT YOUR SWING TO A TEE

Controlling trajectory off the tee is just as important as it is on approach shots, especially on par-3 holes. You can give yourself a great start on producing the shot trajectory you want simply by adjusting how you tee the ball. If you're going for a high shot, tee the ball slightly higher than you normally would. Assuming you make a good swing, you'll hit the ball a little higher on the clubface, with most of the mass of the golf club below the equator of the golf ball. Likewise, when you want to hit the ball low, tee it down so that the ball is just barely above the grass of the tee box.

These slight variations do more than physically assist you in creating the shot you need. They send a message to your brain, letting it know the desired result. If you've practiced the techniques described in this chapter, something as simple as adjusting the height of the tee will help trigger your brain to make the necessary adjustments.

You can use the height of the tee to "program" the height of your shots on par-3 holes.

DON'T LET THE WIND BLOW YOU AWAY

I don't know any golfer who doesn't have to deal with windy conditions from time to time. I've always felt that you could tell a lot about a player's abilities by how he or she responds to difficult conditions, and there is nothing tougher on the golf course than a stiff breeze. While you may be able to get away with some shotmaking inconsistencies in perfect weather, the wind will exaggerate and expose most any flaw. To conquer it, you have to strike the ball cleanly and understand how to affect its flight.

In a moment we'll take a look at how to play different types of wind shots, but there are a few common setup elements that all wind shots require.

- Widen your stance by two to four inches, depending on the wind, for additional stability during the swing, and flex your knees a little more than usual to lower your center of gravity.

- Grip down on the club an inch or two to give yourself better control of the golf club.

- Play the ball back in your stance one or two inches to encourage a hitting position in which your hands are in front of the clubhead at impact.

Now just make sure you stay relaxed as you play the shot.

Downwind With the possible exception of the tee shot, I believe it's best to play low shots when the wind is behind you. With short iron shots, the wind can knock the ball down or take away backspin. You don't need to make any special swing adjustments when playing downwind—but make sure you've modified your setup as described above. Club down, taking about one less club for every ten miles per hour of wind. Concentrate on good tempo. Then just play your own game without trying to overpower the ball. The wind will add the extra yards.

Into the Wind   When playing into the wind, it's important to hit shots with low, boring trajectories, avoiding the rising shot that tends to balloon as the wind gets underneath it. Apply the ten miles per hour rule, this time taking more club according to the wind speed. As you prepare to play the shot, visualize a low trajectory. If the wind is gusting strongly, exaggerate the knockdown shot. Move the ball another inch or two back in your stance and position your hands a little farther ahead of the ball. Firm up your grip pressure slightly. This will help you keep the ball down by inhibiting a full arm and wrist release through the hitting area. The swing should be smooth, with a three-quarters backswing and a low, three-quarters follow-through. Make sure you use enough club and have a smooth, slower forward swing tempo to keep the ball from spinning. Lower clubhead speed produces less spin.

Crosswind   While tour professionals will often try to work the ball into a crosswind, most golfers would have more success with a different method. Simply play the wind to your advantage. Hit the ball into the wind and let it work back on its own. Be sure to align yourself to allow for the wind to move the ball back toward the target. Once more, tempo is the key to keeping the shot from getting away from you, and as we've discussed, a low shot has more control than a high one. The idea is to use the wind, not fight it. Don't think about getting the shot close unless the pin position naturally allows it. Now make a smooth swing and rely on the wind to shape the shot.

By making these slight adjustments to your setup, swing and game plan, you'll stay more relaxed and comfortable in windy conditions. The biggest key to success in the wind is to stay composed and not get anxious. Rarely will you find a perfectly calm day on the golf course, and wind is difficult for all players. However, with a good attitude and a little knowledge of shotmaking, you can prevent it from blowing your golf game away.

Chapter Summary

THE LOW SHOT

Setup

- Use one more club (e.g., if the distance calls for a 6-iron, use a 5-iron to hit a low shot)

- Grip down one to two inches, move one to two inches closer to the ball

- Firm up grip pressure

- Shoulders almost level at address—upper body on top of lower body

- Ball position in center of stance

- Set hands slightly ahead of ball

Swing

- Three-quarters backswing

- Stay level through the hitting area

- Lead with your hands, resisting release

- Rotate body fully to the target

- Low finish with hands, arms and golf club

Strategy

- Setup and swing decreases the effective loft of the club you're using

- Plan for more roll than normal

- Great shot in windy conditions

- Rehearse the shot, especially if swing may be restricted

- Visualize the low trajectory of the shot

Swing Thoughts

- A low shot requires a low finish

- Focus on keeping the hands ahead of the ball through the hitting area

THE HIGH SHOT

Setup

- Use one more club (e.g., if the distance calls for a 6-iron, use a 5-iron to hit a high shot)

- Position ball one inch forward of normal

- Increase your spine tilt by lowering the right shoulder at address

- Weight favors the right side slightly

- Setup adjustments open clubface slightly, adding loft

Swing

- Long, smooth swing with full shoulder turn and body pivot on the backswing

- Allow the forward swing to work along the shoulder tilt established at address

- Feel as though your weight is staying back on the right side

- Let hands release fully through the hitting area

- High finish with hands, arms and golf club

Strategy

- Examine the lie; this shot may not work if ball is sitting down or on hardpan

- Setup and swing adjustments increase the effective loft of the club you're using

- Won't roll as much as a normal shot

- A must shot for hitting over trees or other obstacles

- Rehearse the shot imaging the trajectory and ball flight

Swing Thoughts

- Stay behind the ball

- A high shot requires a high finish

- Allow the right shoulder to "work under" to add loft and height to the shot

Practice Strategies

LOW AND HIGH SHOTS

The golden rule of shotmaking: You should only attempt to pull off a shot in competition that you have experience with in practice. Use the following practice ideas to help you build confidence when it comes to going over or under an obstacle on the golf course.

Fundamental Drill

Use the range setting to practice controlling the trajectory of your shots. Use your imagination to set up shots that require a high trajectory or a low one. Perhaps you may envision a tall tree you need to fly the ball over, or low branches you need to punch under. Use the setup adjustments and swing keys provided in this chapter to help you create these shots on the range. Use different clubs to explore your limitations. For example, just how high can you hit a 4-iron?

When possible, use situations on the golf course to practice negotiating obstacles by hitting over and then under them. Which strategy works best for your style of play? Be sure to hit high and low shots from different lies. How much does the lie affect your ability to pull off the shot?

Competitive Drill

Use the five-ball drill to master trajectory control. Start with either your odd or even clubs for the first practice session, then switch it up the next time on the range. Choose four clubs that represent the different amounts of loft in your bag (e.g., the even clubs: PW, 8-iron, 4-iron, and 4-wood). Select a target on the range and hit three of five acceptable high shots and three of five acceptable low shots with each club in the series to the same target. Like all the shots in this book, it's important to be able to dial in the right distance and be fairly accurate as you learn to control trajectory. Keep score and a running tally of your personal best.

THREE

THE LONG BALL

And Other Tee Box Tips

"Grip it and rip it."
—John Daly

When it comes to satisfaction on the golf course, there's nothing like hitting a drive right on the sweet spot. You might wonder what driving has to do with scrambling, but in fact the long ball is a vital element of managing your game, which is what this book is really all about. When applied wisely, a few extra yards off the tee can put you in position to hit par-5 holes in two or drive the green on a par-4. And on a day when everything is just a little off, making smart decisions on the tee box can make the difference between playing your second shot from the fairway or from the deep rough. In this chapter, you'll learn how to get that valuable added distance from your driver. You'll also learn how to make good club selection off the tee. The driver isn't always the right choice, even when you're playing for distance.

FEATURED SHOT: THE LONG BALL

A big drive in a timely situation is one of golf's oldest and best weapons. Bobby Jones played a control game but knew that par-5s could make the difference between an average round and a good one. When he stepped up on the tee of a reachable par-5, he could dig for something extra to set up an almost sure birdie. Long hitters have always captured the imagination of the golfing public. Sam Snead, Arnold Palmer, Jack Nicklaus, Jim Dent, John Daly and Tiger Woods all wowed fans first with their power.

The key to making the long ball work in your favor is to know when to reach for it. Start by looking for a wide landing area. It doesn't matter how long a hole is—if your drive costs you a shot, then you've made a poor decision off the tee. At the 1999 British Open at Carnoustie, most of the players were hitting irons off the tee at the 467-yard par-4 17th. It wasn't that they would rather have a 2-iron shot into the green than a 5-iron. It was simply that the punishment for an errant tee shot was too great. The 2-iron approach was favorable to a drop from the water and a 5-iron third shot.

Conversely, long hitters routinely "let the shaft out" at the par-5 15th at Augusta National Golf Club. That's because there's little penalty for a mishit shot. And the reward for catching it pure is great— a mid-iron or short-iron approach and a chance at an eagle.

Once you have committed to the long ball, there are a few adjustments you need to make in both your setup and your swing to increase your chances of hitting it long, right down the fairway.

Setup Changes

Tee the ball a little higher than you normally would. In order to create maximum distance with the driver, you want to catch the ball slightly on the upswing and increase the launch angle for more carry. Teeing the ball higher will also prevent you from hitting down into the ball, imparting backspin and decreasing distance.

Widen your stance. The long-ball swing is going to generate more torque and more speed, so you need to have a stable foundation that will support the additional motion and speed and will allow you to maintain balance throughout the swing. Your stance should be slightly wider than your shoulders, with your weight positioned on the balls of your feet and slightly more weight on the right side.

Play the ball up in your stance, about an inch in front of the left heel, again helping to set up an impact position in which you are striking the ball just on the upswing. Your hands should be just behind the ball. Set up with your right shoulder lower than usual to help your body stay more behind the ball throughout the swing and into impact. Use a light

Power begins in the setup, with a wide stance, the ball played forward and the hands just behind the ball.

grip pressure in both hands to encourage a longer, tension-free backswing and to encourage good hand action through the hitting area.

Finally, align yourself for a draw. A right-to-left shot adds overspin that will give you valuable yards on the ground. Close your stance slightly and align your body along the stance line. See the "The Draw" section of chapter 1 (page 8) for more information on drawing the ball.

Swing Changes

The key to added distance is making a longer backswing that will give you more time to build clubhead speed as you swing down into impact. You also want to make as wide a swing as possible. You do this by increasing your upper-body turn while keeping your arms extended from your body. Greg Norman has a fantastic wide swing arc. That is one of the main reasons he is still able to hit the ball out there with the young players on the Tour. Some players, including Norman, Jack Nicklaus and Tiger Woods, also "hover" the clubhead above the ground at address. They claim that this allows them to extend their arms more on the takeaway and also reduces tension in the hands and arms. Give it a try on the practice tee and see if it works for you.

As for the swing itself, you should swing at your normal tempo on the backswing. Maintain your wide arc at the top of the swing, with your arms extended and your hands as far away from your body as you

A wide arc on the takeaway helps initiate a strong turn and a long backswing.

At the top, your arms should be extended and your hands should be well away from your body.

Stay behind the ball with your upper body on the forward swing, and let it rip!

can get them. The torque of your body and the arc of the swing are responsible for the power you will generate on the forward swing.

When you are really looking to hit the ball hard, you need to make a faster forward swing with arms and body. Be aware of your transition into the forward swing. The acceleration of the clubhead must be gradual in order to be controlled. Concentrate on maintaining balance—you want to swing through the ball as fast and hard as you can while still staying in balance. Stay behind the ball to set up an impact position where you contact the ball just as the clubhead begins to move upward, past its bottom point. Maintain your spine angle as you swing into the hitting area. It's very easy to jump at the ball when you're putting something extra into it. Your finish should be well balanced, with your weight on the outside of your left foot and your belt buckle rotated to face slightly left of the target.

SELECTING THE RIGHT DRIVER

No matter how far you hit the ball or what your ball flight tendencies are, there's a driver out there that promises to give you 10–15 extra yards. The problem is that you have to find it. If you're looking for a new driver, you need to take several design factors into consideration.

Start with the shaft. Matching shaft weight and flex to your swing is the single most important element in getting maximum distance. There are no standards, so shaft fitting is often a matter of trying many different combinations of weight and flex. For golfers who don't generate high clubhead speed, an ultralight graphite shaft can be a great help. These shafts weigh in at just 45 to 60 grams, lowering the overall weight of the club and placing most of that weight in the clubhead. If you already have a good deal of power, however, ultralight shafts can disrupt your tempo and timing. Flex is a very individual matter as well. Don't make the mistake of selecting a shaft flex based only on clubhead speed. While it's true that faster clubhead speeds generally match up with stiffer shafts, the key to shaft fitting is how your swing loads and unloads energy. For example, Fred Couples often uses a 3-wood with a ladies' shaft because it matches his rhythm and tempo.

Some clubmakers are manufacturing drivers in lengths of 45, 46 and even 47 inches. The theory is that a longer club will generate greater clubhead speed. While this is true on paper, swinging a longer club won't provide extra distance if you don't hit the ball in the center of the clubface. My advice is to stick with a more conventional length—43.5 or 44 inches—and work on the techniques described in this chapter to get your added distance.

Head materials are another factor you should consider in your driver purchase. Titanium is very popular among designers because they can use it to build larger clubheads with thinner faces while maintaining structural integrity. Titanium is significantly lighter than steel, so some manufacturers now supplement the titanium heads with tungsten or steel weights to lower the center of gravity of the driver and help golfers get the ball in the air more easily. Titanium by itself won't help you hit the ball any farther, but combined with a longer, lighter shaft, some golfers—again, especially those with slower swing speeds—may find extra yards and more forgiving mishits. Of course, titanium is very expensive as well. This added cost and a lack of proven performance benefits have led to a resurgence of stainless steel drivers.

Finally, think about the loft of the driver. Many golfers simply equate loft with distance. If a driver with nine degrees of loft goes a certain distance, then a driver with only seven degrees of loft should go even farther. This line of reasoning is badly flawed. Loft is a dynamic function of the club. In other words, the loft of the clubface at address may not be the same as the effective loft of the face at impact. All the design features already listed can play into effective loft, as well as angle of attack on the forward swing.

My advice is to try as many drivers as you can. When you find one that consistently gives you good trajectory and accuracy, go with it. If you practice, you can always get a few extra yards when you need them. But a driver that gives you the confidence that you can hit the fairway is a dangerous club indeed.

Have a Ball

Also, don't forget that you have a choice of golf ball designs as well. Low-handicappers and professionals are more concerned with feel and spin for shotmaking control and tend to use softer wound or multi-cover ball designs. If you're a mid- or high-handicapper, however, you should try a harder, two-piece ball that spins less. Reduced spin will help you hit it not only longer but straighter as well, since a two-piece distance ball reduces both backspin and sidespin.

Cover materials and thickness and the core of the ball all affect its playability. I encourage you to experiment with different types of balls in different weather and course conditions. If there's an advantage to be gained, you should be familiar enough with equipment technology to gain it.

Driving with the Wind

You're standing on the tee box of a 300-yard par-4 with the wind at your back. You can hardly wait to tee up your driver and just let it rip. Well, here's a secret—your driver may not always be the longest club in your bag.

When you're driving with the wind and you want to get maximum distance, the best way to take full advantage of the tailwind is to get the ball high up into the air. In this situation, you are better off using your 3-wood.

Tee the ball just slightly higher than a nice fairway lie. The only setup changes you should make are to move the ball forward slightly, about one inch in front of where you would normally play it for a 3-wood shot and increase your spine tilt so that more weight is on your right side at address.

As you swing, concentrate on staying behind the ball. The additional loft of the 3-wood imparts more backspin, helping the ball naturally fly higher than a driver. Once it's up, your ball will ride the wind and should travel farther than any shot you could hit with a driver. Try it. It works.

Conditioning

If you're really serious about adding distance to your drives, your swing adjustments must be accompanied by better physical conditioning. If you wonder how Tiger Woods and Sergio Garcia can be among the longest hitters in the game, given their thin physiques, the answer lies in conditioning. They have both invested a lot of time in building the muscle groups that affect distance—the shoulders, forearms, hands, lower back and legs. They also are very flexible.

A number of good golf conditioning books have appeared recently. These books include exercises and stretches to help tune your body to produce greater clubhead speed. Pick one up and start a personal conditioning program—especially during the off-season.

Driving Strategies

Too many golfers approach driving the ball with a one-dimensional game plan—maximum distance. You would never use that thinking on your iron shots to the green, and you shouldn't use it off the tee, either. Your tee shots can make the difference between a round with many scoring opportunities and a round where you spend all your time hunting for balls, playing shots from deep rough and counting penalty strokes.

By now you should know your game and your tendencies pretty well. If you tend to hook the ball when you are not hitting it well, don't try for extra yards on any hole where there is trouble on the left. In the same way that altering your swing magnifies distance when you hit the ball solidly, it also magnifies mistakes. Keep this in mind as you make your decisions.

If you watch golf on television, you've heard the analysts talk about driving in terms of the angle of approach the drive leaves the player. This is a great way to start thinking of your own drives. On most holes, the approach to the green is much easier from one side of the fairway than the other. Maybe there's a large bunker guarding the left side of the green that hardly comes into play from the right side. This is vital information to know as you stand on the tee box.

The most important thing you can do to improve your driving is to have a distinct target area of the fairway in mind. The target area should provide you with the most open approach to the green or pin. It should also play to your strengths. In other words, if you aren't confident with your 110-yard shot, your target area on a short par-4 should leave you at a distance and line where you are more comfortable. Don't think of irons off the tee as only "layups." Make your club selection based on the target area you have selected. If you have chosen a target area that is 200 yards from the tee, and that will leave you with a desirable 130-yard shot to the green as well as taking a fairway bunker out of play, you're not laying up by hitting an iron. You're hitting a smart drive.

You may have also heard announcers pointing out how the tour professionals use the entire tee box. This is another sign of an advanced player. Many weekend golfers simply tee the ball up in the middle of the tee box and swing away. Instead, you should choose the side of the tee box that gives you the best angle of approach to your target area. The tee box is the only part of the golf course where you get to choose the line of your next shot. This is a giant mental and physical advantage over any other shot you will encounter during the round. Take full advantage. If your target area is in the left side of the fairway, and you like to draw the ball, tee up on the left side of the tee box so you can start the ball out to the right and work it back into the target. If you're a straight ball hitter, you may choose to play from the right side of the tee box to reach the same target area. In that case, the right side would give you more room for error.

Remember, the key to good driving is to look at it not as a distance contest but as a chance to set up your next shot. If you do that, you'll soon develop a feel for tee shots, and you'll know when it's safe to try for a little added distance.

Chapter Summary

THE LONG TEE-BALL

Setup

- Tee the ball a little higher than normal to catch the ball on the upswing

- Widen stance to slightly wider than the shoulders to support a longer, faster swing

- Play the ball one inch forward of normal driver position

- Set up with shoulders square to the target line, but with an increased tilt to lower the right shoulder a bit to set up behind the ball, and to help keep your weight behind the ball on the forward swing

- Use light grip pressure for a full release of hands and club through the hitting area

- Close the stance slightly to set up for a draw—see chapter 1

Swing

- Let the club swing straight back for the first foot to encourage a wide swing arc

- Swing at a normal tempo on the backswing but a slightly faster pace on the forward swing

- Make a full body pivot around the right leg

- Maintain the wide arc established at the takeaway throughout the backswing

- At the top of the swing, make sure arms are fully extended in front of the chest—swing may feel a little shorter

- Stay behind the ball as you make the forward swing

- Make a full, well-balanced finish

Strategy

- Hit it long off the tee only if you have a wide landing area—extra distance won't help if it costs you a shot to recover

- Consider your directional misses with the driver—a longer, faster swing magnifies sidespin and the amount of curve

- Have your professional help you determine if your driver has the appropriate shaft weight, length, flex and loft for your swing

- If distance is a primary objective, use a harder, two-piece ball that spins less

Swing Thoughts

- Start and stay relaxed for maximum body rotation and clubhead speed

- Smooth tempo and even rhythm is key—avoid jumping at the ball from the top

Practice Strategies

THE LONG BALL

Let's face it, golf has become a power game. The players on the pro tours who can knock the ball out of sight have a huge advantage over the field. A longer tee shot means you have a shorter iron into the green—and pinpoint accuracy is much easier with a more lofted club. On the pro tours if you can't keep up in reaching the par-5s in two, you're giving shots to the field. Besides, I don't know many golfers, pro or amateur, who wouldn't like to hit the ball longer. Not only does it make the game easier, it makes the game more fun. All it takes is a little practice to squeeze a few extra yards out of your driver.

Fundamental Drill

Be sure you work on hitting the long ball only after a sufficient warm-up. You want to get the most out of your practice and to avoid injury. If you don't already have a pretty good idea of your driving average, start by charting the next couple of rounds. Once you know the distance you hit your driver on average, use the setup and swing adjustments in this chapter to step it up. Have fun hitting drives and really letting it rip. If you watch kids on the range, they're trying to push the envelope on power and you should take their lead. Try to see how fast you can swing while being able to maintain balance. Start out by making five practice swings—fast and in balance. Then rip a drive, holding a balanced finish until the ball hits the ground. You can also try the "swoosh" drill. Turn your driver upside down, holding it in your right hand just below the clubhead. Make five swings trying to create a loud swoosh at the bottom of the swing. Then hit some drives trying to create the same fast clubhead speed. As you try to hit the ball farther, monitor your grip pressure. Do you do better using a slightly lighter grip pressure? Can you still hit the ball relatively straight even when you're amping up the clubhead speed? Finally, take advantage of the demo drivers in your club's shop to experiment with different shafts, shaft flexes, shaft lengths and amounts of loft. You need to discover the driver that produces the launch conditions that maximize your driving distance.

FOUR

THE
FEATHERED IRON
No-Man's-Land—Between Clubs

*"You can't hit a good five-iron when you're thinking
about a six-iron on your backswing."*
—Charles Coody

In 1998, Fred Couples held the lead as he came to the 13th tee in the final round of the Masters. A former champion at Augusta National, he looked to be in complete control of the tournament. Then he hooked his drive badly, winding up to the left of Rae's Creek. He couldn't go for the green in two, of course, but, still, things didn't look too bad. He hit a wedge safely back to the fairway. From there he had 165 yards to the pin. Fred put his hand first on his 7-iron. Then he moved it to the 6-iron. He debated for a long while. The problem was that the shot he faced was right in-between clubs. Should he take less club and hit the ball harder or more club and take something off it? Finally he decided to take the longer club and hit a softer shot. He planned to take something off the 6-iron, hitting a high, left-to-right shot. Then he made a mistake I've seen hundreds of players make. He quit on the shot. The ball started to the right and stayed there, splashing into the creek beside the green. The resulting double-bogey cost him the lead, and he never got it back.

Golf is a game of finesse and touch, two qualities Fred Couples has in abundance. And yet even with his relaxed, rhythmic swing, he let this partial shot get away from him. Getting stuck between clubs is a common occurrence, whether you're trying to win the Masters or playing a friendly weekend round. To maximize your scoring potential, you have to know how to squeeze an extra five or ten yards out of a certain club or how to gear down to hit that same club five to ten yards shorter than usual.

Sam Snead says he can hit any club in his bag between 50 and 200 yards, including his putter. That kind of distance control is crucial to good shotmaking. In the days before accurate yardage markers on golf courses took the guesswork out of distance, Snead earned a reputation for gamesmanship thanks to his uncanny control of his swing. If he sensed an opponent trying to gain an advantage by figuring out what club he was using, Snead would throw him off by choosing much more club than necessary and feathering the shot or choosing less club and hitting it farther. Today, club selection trickery is not as much a part of the game, but that doesn't mean you shouldn't know how to manage the distances of your shots. Just as you need to have the ability to work the ball to the right or to the left, you also need to be able to stretch or reduce the yardage you get out of any club.

Tour pros today seem to prefer using three-quarters swings and knockdowns for better distance control and accuracy. In fact, many play partial shots almost exclusively when approaching the green with a middle iron or short iron. Why? The mechanics of the partial shot tend to produce a lower, flatter trajectory that is much easier to predict than a high, soaring shot.

SWINGERS VS. HITTERS

The first step you can take toward becoming more confident when you find yourself between clubs is to determine what type of player you are. I divide golfers into two categories: swingers and hitters. Swingers have longer, slower swings. Think of Ernie Els, Fred Couples or Meg Mallon. Hitters, on the other hand, have fast, accelerating swings that really explode through the ball. Nick Price and Tiger Woods are both classic hitters.

In general, swingers prefer to use a longer club and take a little something off a shot when between clubs. Since Fred Couples is a very smooth swinger of the club, I think he made the right mental decision in that Masters tournament. Unfortunately, he failed to execute. Hitters will almost always take the shorter club and add a few yards to it. Both strategies can be very effective, but only when applied properly to a player's swing and temperament. Think back—have you ever seen Tiger Woods try to ease up on a shot?

Knowing what type of player you are will help you make better shotmaking decisions when playing partial shots and will allow you to play the shot you've selected with more confidence. How do you tell which camp you belong to? If you don't already know, all you need to do is pay attention. The kind of player you are—a swinger or a hitter—should be readily apparent. Do you focus on smoothness and accuracy or do you play a power game? The best golfers know that some rounds require you to be a little of both types of player, depending on the day and the circumstances.

MAKING THE RIGHT DECISION

In addition to your natural swing, other factors can contribute to your decision to use a longer club or a shorter club when you're stuck in the middle.

Factors That Favor the Longer Club

- There is trouble short of the green. A shot that flies farther would not jeopardize a good score as much as one that comes up short.

- The flagstick is toward the front of the green, accessible only with a high, soft shot.

- You're a higher handicap golfer who tends to come up short of the green.

- The shot is uphill.

Factors That Favor the Shorter Club

- The front of the green is open enough to receive a low shot.

- The flagstick is toward the back of the green, giving you plenty of room to hit a shot that comes in low and running.

- You play with a little power in reserve and can call up those extra few yards when you need them.

- The shot is downhill.

- You hit the ball solidly most of the time and know how to shape shots when you need to.

- You're in a pressure situation, and your adrenaline is pumping.

FEATURED SHOT: THE FEATHERED IRON— TAKING FIVE TO TEN YARDS OFF

Unless you are a very strong player, I would recommend that the soft approach shot—the feathered iron—is the safest and most useful shot to use when you are between clubs. Since the swing is smoother and slower, you have a better chance of hitting the ball solidly—the most important element in all shotmaking.

You can hit this shot with any club, including your woods. If you have a utility wood such as a 7-wood or 5-wood, you'll find that it's particularly useful for soft shots. Take one more club than normal, grip down one or two inches and stand slightly closer to the ball. The shorter handle will give you a shorter swing arc and will reduce club-head speed while still letting you stay with the shot all the way through the hitting area. Use your normal grip pressure in both hands. This keeps you tension-free and allows you to feel the clubhead throughout the swing. Ball position is the same as for a shot of regular length. Set your hands in a neutral position, even with the ball.

Make a three-quarters arm swing going back. Let the lower body

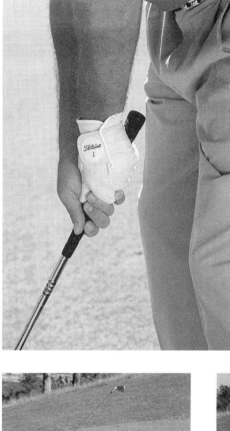

Grip down on the club when you want to reduce clubhead speed to hit a soft shot.

Make your swing an equal length back and through.

turn in response to the upper body on the backswing. The shorter backswing helps take something off the shot. The tempo of the forward swing is a little slower than normal. Concentrate on making solid contact. The forward swing should be the same length as the backswing. Check your finish. Your weight will be all the way over to your left side, and your body rotated around to face the target. Good balance is the key. If you're having trouble keeping your balance at the finish of this shot, work more on the pace of the overall swing and particularly the transition between backswing and forward swing.

A second way to hit a soft approach shot is to open the clubface slightly and play a high fade. See the section on fading the ball in chapter 1. This can be a great solution when you are between clubs but need to produce a high shot that will stop when it lands.

THE HOT APPROACH: GETTING AN EXTRA FIVE TO TEN YARDS

I tend to see more hitters these days than I do swingers, especially among the men I work with. They are in good shape and produce a very high clubhead speed. When these players find themselves between clubs, my advice is usually to take the shorter club and squeeze a little more out of it. I believe that everyone can get five to ten extra yards out of any club using these techniques.

Use the shorter club. If you were choosing between a 7-iron and an 8-iron, go with the 8-iron. Hold the club at the end of the handle. Maintain a lighter grip pressure to encourage a full hand release. Now widen your stance slightly. To get more out of a shot, you're going to have to put a little more into it. A wider stance provides a strong foundation to support a longer and faster swing.

Set up with the ball about an inch back in your stance, with your hands set forward, just ahead of the ball. These adjustments close the clubface slightly, de-lofting the club to produce a lower trajectory and to add that little bit of distance you need.

Use a backswing that is a little longer than normal. Concentrate on

To get extra yards from an iron, play the ball back and hood the clubface slightly with your hands set forward.

You'll need a bigger backswing, with a good upper-body turn, to get that added distance.

making a good, full shoulder turn, bringing your left shoulder underneath your chin. You'll need a faster forward swing tempo than you usually use. You don't have to try to kill the ball, but you do have to promote a swing that delivers higher clubhead speed than your normal swing. Swing into a well-balanced finish.

Again, there are several ways to get more yards out of a club. The longer, faster swing I've described above is the way I would recommend to most people, but I've seen other methods work very well. Some golfers simply close the face of the club at address and allow for right-to-left movement of the ball. Making the standard adjustments for a draw (see "The Draw" in chapter 1) is a very good way to add a little bit of distance. Just remember that curving the ball is not always feasible or desirable. The cardinal rule of all shotmaking is knowing your options.

Using Partial Shots

It's no secret that over the past few years players have gotten stronger and longer. Tiger Woods, Justin Leonard, Davis Love, Sergio Garcia, Karrie Webb—all of these players generate amazing clubhead speed even though they have slight builds. While this ability to whip the clubhead through the ball at speeds of 115 miles per hour or more is a great asset off the tee, it can be problematic on approach shots. In order to gain control over their distance and trajectories, these strong players often use a three-quarters shot as their standard approach.

Watch Tiger Woods play, and you'll see that even though he's using a partial swing on many of his iron shots, he isn't slowing down the swing—he simply shortens his arm swing in both directions and then fires at full speed. The resulting ball flight resembles a knockdown, traveling with a low, flat trajectory.

If you have trouble with controlling the distance of your shots—especially the short irons—you may want to try this strategy. Grip down at least one inch on the handle of the club and hold the club firmly in both hands. The shorter lever serves to decrease clubhead speed and make the club easier to control. Play the ball in the middle of your stance. Swing the club three-quarters of the way back using your normal swing speed. Again, make sure to be smooth on the transition between the backswing and forward swing, but swing into impact at full speed, and finish in a three-quarters position.

An abbreviated follow-through can help control distance and accuracy, even on a full-tempo swing.

Making this your go-to shot can help you hit more greens in regulation and give yourself more birdie opportunities. When it comes to approach shots, hitting the ball as far as you can is not always a good strategy.

Remember, distance is a function of loft control, length of the club, the swing and pace of the swing. If you work on these three elements, you'll be able to handle any between-clubs situation.

Chapter Summary

THE FEATHERED IRON

Setup

- Use the longer club when a particular yardage puts you between two clubs (e.g., if you're between a 6-iron and a 5-iron, use the 5-iron)

- Grip down one to two inches

- Ball position same as for a regular shot

Swing

- Three-quarters backswing and forward swing

- Let the lower body turn in response to the upper body in the backswing

- Tempo of the forward swing is a little slower than normal

- The shorter length swing creates a shorter swing arc, which means decreased clubhead speed and decreased distance

Advanced Techniques

- Open clubface slightly and hit a high fade—see "Featured Shot: The Fade" in chapter 1

Strategy

- If you have trouble deciding whether to add or subtract yardage from a shot, bear in mind that the following situations favor the soft approach: 1) you tend to be swinger, not a hitter, 2) there's trouble short of the green, 3) the pin is toward the front of the green, 4) you are a high handicapper

- Know how much yardage the soft approach generally takes off

- Decide on the shot and commit fully to executing it

Swing Thoughts

- Swing with a smooth, slightly slower forward swing tempo

- Make solid contact

THE HOT APPROACH

Setup

- Use the shorter club when a particular yardage puts you between two clubs (e.g., if you're between a 6-iron and a 5-iron, use the 6-iron)

- Hold the club at the end of the grip

- Employ a lighter than normal grip pressure in both hands to encourage a full release

- Stance slightly wider than normal

- Ball position one to two inches back, with hands set slightly forward to de-loft the club

Swing

- Use a backswing that is a little longer than normal

- Make a full and complete shoulder turn behind the ball

- Tempo of the forward swing is a little faster than normal

- Make a complete, balanced finish

Advanced Techniques

- Close the clubface slightly and hit a draw—see "The Draw" in chapter 1.

Strategy

- If you have trouble deciding on whether to add or subtract yardage from a shot, bear in mind that the following situations favor the hot approach: 1) you tend to be hitter, not a swinger, 2) there's no trouble to carry in front of the green, 3) the pin is toward the back of the green, 4) you're a low handicapper who makes solid contact most times, 5) your normal swing has a little power in reserve, 6) you're in a pressure situation and your adrenaline is pumping

- Know how much yardage the hot approach generally adds

- Decide on the shot and commit fully to executing it

Swing Thoughts

- Big upper-body turn

- Longer arm swing

- Faster forward-swing tempo

Practice Strategies

BETWEEN CLUBS

You face many shots during a round that don't exactly correspond to the yardage you hit a particular club. Knowing whether you perform best by using more club and taking a little off, or less club and squeezing a few extra yards, will help you execute such a shot with confidence.

Fundamental Drill

Choose a target on the range that is typically between the yardage you hit one of your clubs. Most good practice ranges have several targets with posted yardages, so it should be relatively easy to identify one. Let's say you found a target at 155 yards which is exactly between the distance you hit your 7-iron and your 6-iron. Using the setup and swing adjustments of the soft approach, try to hit the 6-iron 5 to 10 yards shorter to hit the target. Monitor the length and pace of your swing as you try to strike the ball solidly. Then move down and hit your 7-iron and make the setup and swing adjustments to squeeze a few extra yards. Do you have the strength and clubhead speed to take this approach? Which approach allows you to have better control of your golf club? Experiment with closing the face of your 7-iron slightly to see if this produces the necessary added yardage. Then try opening the face of your 6-iron slightly to hit a soft fade. How accurate are you with each series of balls? Answering these questions will help you determine the approach that's most natural when you are between clubs.

Competitive Drill

After you've experimented with both methods of adding or subtracting yards with your clubs, use the five-ball drill to keep score and put a little pressure on your shots. Keep a tally to see how successful you are at scoring three out five acceptable shots with each approach. What method allows you to score the most points? Keep track in your practice journal to see whether you develop a consistent pattern.

FIVE

THE FLYER

And Other Truths About Lies

"I catch fish in water shallower than the rough here."
—Phil Blackmar

In the final round of the 1998 U.S. Open at the Olympic Club in San Francisco, Payne Stewart was scrambling his way to par after par, clinging tenaciously to the lead he had held since the opening round. His short game had been his best friend all week. Finally, shortly after making the turn into the home stretch, hit a perfect drive at the par-4 12th hole, straight down the middle of the fairway. When he got to his ball, however, he got a rude surprise. The best tee shot he had hit all day had come to rest squarely in a sand-filled divot. Payne now faced a 9-iron shot of some 145 yards. Needless to say, it was a tough pill to swallow. He ended up catching the ball heavy, leaving it in a greenside bunker and failing to get up and down for par. Just when it looked like he would have a little breather, the golf course had thrown him a curve.

Sound familiar? I'm sure you have found yourself in plenty of situations in which the shot you were faced with would have been much easier if you'd only caught a perfect lie. There's a term for what happened to Payne that day and for what has happened to every player who has hit an apparently good shot that ultimately landed them in a tough situation—rub of the green.

There's no way of preventing rub of the green, but in terms of handling imperfect lies, there is often a cure. A little knowledge and technique can go a long way. Over the next few pages, we'll take a look at some of the troublesome lies you frequently encounter on the golf course. These include flyer lies caused by rough or wet grass, lies in which the ball is sitting down in moderate rough, heavy rough lies, divots and hardpan. And all of them are very much playable. Golfers who know how to score understand how to carefully evaluate a lie, design a strategy based on the conditions, select the proper club for the shot and make a swing that is well within their capabilities. You can do all of those things as well. And while you may not be able to eliminate the effects of a difficult lie, you'll certainly be able to minimize the damage—and hit a few heroic shots as well.

One of the most basic things you can do to improve your play from different lies is simply to be aware of your surroundings. What are the lies that you encounter most frequently? Take note of the seasonal changes at your home course and practice accordingly. In the winter or early spring, you may see a number of hardpan lies on the course while in summer the rough may have totally different characteristics. As with any golf situation, familiarity is your greatest asset.

Once you've made your mental notes regarding the lies you can expect on the course, integrate those lies into your practice routine. Too many golfers practice incorrectly, hitting only certain clubs from ideal lies. Reserve time toward the end of your practice sessions to work on the techniques and situations described in this chapter.

WHAT CAN A LIE TELL YOU?

The lie of the ball can take a lot of guesswork out of your shotmaking decisions. The lie determines how "cleanly" you can strike the ball with the clubface. Golf is often a game of millimeters, and a few blades of grass between the ball and clubface at impact can make a dramatic difference in the behavior of the shot. Likewise, deeper grass might affect your ability to maintain a square clubface through the hitting area because it wraps itself around the clubhead as you try to swing into the hitting area. Even shots that seem at first impossible to predict, such as shots from divots, will prove to have a pattern once you've hit enough of them.

The situations I've chosen to highlight in this chapter are simply the most common ones, found on just about every golf course. Again, be sure to notice the lies that are unique to the courses you play on. Chances are, the techniques you'll read about over the following pages will help you handle those as well.

FEATURED SHOT: THE FLYER

Have you ever hit a ball into the first cut of rough, just off the fairway, found it sitting up perfectly, congratulated yourself on your good fortune, and then airmailed the green by ten yards with your approach shot? If so, you have already met the flyer lie.

The flyer can lull you to sleep because it looks so inviting at first glance. Any time the ball is sitting up in the rough, watch out for a flyer. Also, if you play in the early morning before the dew has burned off or following an afternoon shower, you may encounter a flyer from anywhere on the course.

The reason we call this shot a flyer is simple—grass or water gets

A flyer lie can result from the ball sitting either up or down in the first cut of rough.

between the ball and clubface and reduces spin. Tour players call it the "Chapstick effect." I've even heard rumors of players intentionally filling the grooves of their drivers with Chapstick to create this kind of flyer effect off the tee, but there's no benefit to a flyer when you're approaching the green. Instead, you'll find your iron shot sailing high and far. If you normally hit a 7-iron 150 yards, you may find yourself easily hitting it 160 or even 170 yards if you catch a flyer.

The single greatest key to neutralizing a flyer situation when the ball is sitting up in the rough or when the grass has water on it is to make setup and swing adjustments that allow you to sweep the ball off the grass.

I teach players to handle flyer lies by making three simple changes. First, drop down a club. Even if you handle the flyer lie cleanly, you'll still be producing a shot that travels farther than it would from a normal lie. Then grip down on the club about an inch. This raises the bottom point of the swing, again encouraging you to sweep the ball. Take a wide stance—about shoulder width—to encourage a shallower angle on the forward swing, and play the ball about an inch forward in your stance, just inside the left heel. From there, make a normal swing. You'll catch the ball just beyond the bottom point of the swing and produce what I call a "controlled flyer."

During the swing, you should concentrate on tempo. Because the ball is going to fly farther, swing at less than full speed on the forward swing. Focus on staying level all the way through impact. The setup and swing adjustments

When the ball is sitting up, you want to set up to "sweep" the ball. That means grip down one inch, take a wider stance and play the ball one inch more forward.

you've made will ensure a level path through the hitting area—the key to sweeping the ball from a flyer lie.

If you're faced with a flyer lie where the ball is sitting down in a first cut of rough, use this same technique, but instead of moving the ball forward in your stance, move it back to the center. This will set you up to make a slightly more descending blow. Take a three-quarters swing, and be aware that the ball will fly a little lower than normal and will run a long way when it lands.

DOWN IN THE ROUGH

Nobody finds the fairway every time. And when summertime rolls around and golf courses are in the best shape they'll be in all year, it's not unusual to have some shots in each round that end up nestled down in the rough. Now, I'm not talking about lies where the ball is totally covered—I'll get to those in a little bit. I'm talking about lies where at least half the ball is above the top of the grass. Though the grass is definitely going to alter the shot, you can still strike the ball with some authority and control.

The problem you face when the ball is sitting down in the rough is that the longer grass is going to "grab" the clubhead before you hit the ball and twist it shut. This grabbing action will cause the shot to come out lower and fly more to the left than a similar shot from the fairway. I wouldn't attempt to hit a ball that is sitting down in the rough with an iron longer than a 4-iron. If the clubface twists too much, you'll end up just rolling the ball along the ground, probably into deeper trouble.

To effectively play a ball that is nestled down into the rough, you need to take steps to minimize the twisting effect of the longer grass. Use one or two clubs more than you normally would to compensate for the decreased distance you'll get playing from thick rough. Grip down one inch for better control and hold the club firmly with both hands—you'll need to hold on to get through the deep grass.

Stand about an inch closer to the ball to initiate a steeper angle on the forward swing and play the ball in the middle of your stance. This will help you strike the ball sooner, before the grass has had a chance to interfere too much with the clubhead.

Now simply set up to hit a fade. Remember, the ball won't curve as much as it would from a clean lie. But the fundamentals of the shot are exactly the same. Align your clubface along the line on which you want the ball to start, with your stance and body opened a corresponding amount and your hands positioned just ahead of the ball. Now swing along the line of your shoulders as you go back, lifting the club more with your arms than you would in a normal swing. The added lift will help you create a steeper angle of attack, a necessity for extracting the ball from the rough. Swing down along the same line, going across the target line. This technique allows you to use the loft of the club to cut through the grass with enough force to strike the ball solidly.

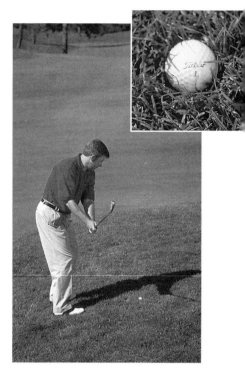

A ball that is sitting well down in the rough will respond to a cut/fade swing.

The idea is to maintain a slightly faster tempo on the forward swing and take a good aggressive pass at the ball. Maintain your grip pressure all the way through the swing. Try to take a divot—this will get you working down into the ball. Rotate all the way through the shot, into a full finish. As you rehearse for the shot, step up the tempo of your forward swing. You'll need all your strength to get the ball out of the long grass and toward your target.

UTILITY WOODS

One of the best things you can do to improve your chances of making good escapes from moderate rough is to replace your longest iron with one of the many utility woods available today. Most tour players carry a 7- or 5-wood to use as a utility club for long shots from the rough. These clubs deliver the distance of a long iron but allow for more shotmaking options.

A wood provides better loft, a lower center of gravity and more surface area at the sole to displace the grass that stands between you and solid contact. Because they have more surface area at the sole-plate, a wood's clubhead and heel are less likely to catch in the grass and shut down prior to impact. The presence of rails or other special soleplate designs on these clubs may deliver even greater performance from tough lies.

Once you get your utility wood, practice with it from all types of lie conditions. You'll find that it's a valuable ally in lots of on-course situations.

Utility woods offer great advantages in the rough. The soleplate of a wood displaces much more grass than an iron.

DEEP ROUGH

Sometimes the rough becomes so severe that it simply swallows the ball, leaving you with few escape routes. The first step in executing a shot in such conditions is to realize that you're in recovery mode. If you're more than 100 yards away from the green, forget about going for it and pick a spot that will afford you the best position for your next shot.

Not only is the grass going to grab the club head and shut the club-face down, but it will significantly slow your clubhead speed as well. In other words, you don't have a whole lot of options.

Prepare for this shot by moving the ball back in your stance, one or two inches right of center. Also, grip down about two inches and stand slightly closer to the ball,, holding the club firmly in both hands, and set your hands in front of the ball. These adjustments will produce a swing that produces a steep angle of attack—the only swing that can result in any reasonable contact between the clubhead and the ball.

Sometimes you just have to take a wedge and dig the ball out and back into play.

Be sure you're using a club with enough loft to get the ball out of trouble and back into a playable position. I usually just go with a short iron when I'm faced with a ball buried in deep rough. Heroic attempts from these situations usually end up being mistakes that cost strokes.

When playing the shot, you want to make a steep arm swing— you should feel as if you're lifting the club directly up—as you swing away from the ball, with little in the way of body turn. Concentrate on tempo as you swing back and then come down on that same steep angle with your hands leading the way. You're not trying to hit it far, just out. Keep your hands and wrists firm through the hitting area and swing the clubhead down into the ground at a steep angle. Your finish will be low, about waist high or just slightly higher. The ball is going to come out low and hot. Allow for nearly half of the total length of the shot to come on the ground.

QUIET PLEASE—REHEARSAL IN PROGRESS

I always encourage golfers, from beginners to Tour players, to use their practice swings as rehearsal for the upcoming shot, particularly when faced with a difficult lie such as moderate or deep rough, hardpan or divots. A conscious rehearsal process is your only opportunity to evaluate how the club is going to react as it swings into unpredictable lies. If your ball is nestled down in moderate or deep rough, take a complete accounting of the situation. Notice whether the grass at your ball is lying with its grain with you or against you, whether it's thick or thin. Now find an area near your ball where you can rehearse in that same situation. Take your practice swings, taking extra care to feel in your hands how the clubface reacts as you swing through the hitting area. This technique helps your mind prepare for the upcoming shot. It's always better to know how the grass is going to affect the clubhead rather than to walk into the shot wondering.

DIVOTS

Divots are just a hard fact of life on the golf course. While no one wants to hit a perfect shot only to find it sitting down in an old divot hole, the shot out of it generally isn't as difficult as you might believe. In fact, I'd say that the most difficult aspect of playing from a divot is to approach the shot with confidence. It looks like you can't possibly have control, but this is an illusion if you make the proper setup and swing adjustments.

First, size up the situation. If the divot is extraordinarily deep and your ball is up against the face of it, you may have to consider whether you want to go for the green or play a layup. But if the divot is of normal size and depth, you just want to make sure that you strike the ball cleanly, letting the loft of the club do the work. Trying to help the ball get into the air by scooping it with your hands and wrists is the last thing you want to try from a divot.

You will probably need to take an extra club, since you'll be making a partial swing. Start by holding the club at the end of the grip with a tighter grip pressure to prevent the clubhead from twisting when it hits the divot. Since the ball is already sitting below ground level, you want to use the full length of the club. Use a little more knee bend, again to lower the bottom point of your swing. Now set up a steep angle of attack on the forward swing by moving the ball back to the center of your stance. This ball position will also set your hands just ahead of the ball.

The swing itself is a three-quarters arm swing driven primarily by the upper body, with minimal lower body coil. If the divot points toward your target, the best key you can use is to swing right down the line of the

Don't let divots panic you. Play the ball back and swing right into the divot hole.

divot. If it points left or right of the target, you still want to swing the club right down the target line—the walls of the divot will give to a good swing. Concentrate on striking the ball first and taking a divot about the depth of the one that's already there. This will help you stay down and through the shot. Keep your wrists firm as you punch through the ball. The finish will be abbreviated even though the body rotates through to face the target.

Fortunately, there's no shortage of divots on most practice ranges. Spend some time working on shots from divots of all shapes and depths. Be sure to hit balls from the front and back of divots to get the feel for how the ball reacts from these different situations. Most of all, approach this shot with confidence. This is one of those situations that can change the course of a round or match. Just when your opponent thinks he's got the upper hand because you're on the wrong side of a bad break, you come back and put the pressure on him. It's a great feeling.

Sanded Divots

If you find yourself in a freshly sanded divot, play the shot more like a fairway bunker shot. Grip down one or two inches on the handle and move the ball slightly back in your stance. Again, don't try to help it into the air. Just concentrate on striking the ball first and letting the loft of the club do the work. Make sure that you stay nice and tall through the entire swing. See "The Fairway Bunker Shot" in chapter 11 for more information.

DIVOTS AND THE RULES

People often ask if divots are considered ground under repair. They're not. Divots are considered an integral part of the golf course. You will never get legitimate relief from a divot. However, there are a couple of notes you should be aware of.

First of all, a divot that has been replaced into a divot hole is deemed to be a part of the golf course. In other words, you can't consider it a loose impediment and move it even if it interferes with your backswing or forward swing. Even if the divot doesn't appear to correspond with the divot hole in which it has been placed, you are not entitled to move the divot at all.

However, if the divot has not been placed in a divot hole and is simply lying on the ground, then it is deemed to be a loose impediment, meaning it can be removed without penalty just like a leaf or a small rock. The distinction between a replaced divot and a loose divot can be a big one. Be sure to check with a rules official or your playing companions if there is any doubt as to whether a divot should be considered "re-placed."

HARDPAN

Thanks to improved course conditioning, you don't see as much hardpan today as players of previous eras did. Hardpan is the term given to patches of dirt or clay that have baked in the sun until becoming extremely hard, sometimes as hard as concrete. Today, we use the term for just about any closely mown area that isn't particularly soft.

Professional golfers love to play full iron shots off hardpan. No other surface maximizes the effects of their precise ball striking. They hit down and through the shot, nipping it off the hardpan with excellent spin and control. To play off hardpan with confidence, I start by taking an extra club. It's important to eliminate any excess motion from your swing in order to hit the ball cleanly. Hold the club at the end of the handle to make it easier for you to swing the clubhead down into the ground. Play the ball back one inch, toward the center of your stance to ensure that you strike the ball first.

Using a backswing controlled by the upper body, make a three-quarters arm swing for added balance. The mistake I most often see with this shot is an uneven transition. Concentrate on making a smooth move from the top of the backswing into the forward swing, leading with your hands as you rotate into and through the hitting area. You'll strike the ball just before the ground. Notice the trajectory you get—it should be nice and flat, with no balloon shape to the shot. This is because you're letting the loft of the club do all the work.

I encourage my students to practice on hardpan at every opportunity. Hardpan requires a smooth, even tempo and a trust of the loft of the golf club and the setup and swing changes you've made. As you feel better about hitting the ball from hardpan, your overall ball-striking will improve.

If you find yourself faced with a pitch shot off hardpan, you're much better off using a punch or a bump-and-run to eliminate the bounce effect that hard ground can have. Because of the bounce effect, I would avoid using your sand or lob wedges when playing from hardpan. The bounce on the flange of your most lofted wedges will increase the possibility of skulling the ball into trouble. Grip down about an inch on the handle and stand an inch closer to the ball to make it easier for you to work the club down into the ball on the forward swing. Play the ball back an inch or two, toward the center of your stance. Use a swing in which the upper body does most of the work with the wrists remaining firm throughout. These adjustments will help make sure that you contact the ball first.

BELIEVE THIS ABOUT LIES

No two lies are ever the same. Integrate various lies into every practice session. As you begin to notice the subtle differences that grasses and ground conditions can make in your ball-striking, you'll begin to truly improve your instincts and capabilities when it comes to handling the wide ranges of lies you encounter during every round of golf.

Chapter Summary

THE FLYER LIE

Setup

- Use one less club (e.g., if the distance calls for a 5-iron, use a 6-iron for this shot)

- Grip down one inch

- Stance slightly wider than normal for shallow angle of approach

- Ball position one inch more forward

- If the ball is in the first cut of rough, but slightly down in the grass, use the same setup adjustments, but move the ball back to the center of the stance to encourage a more descending blow

Swing

- Concentrate on smooth tempo—the lie provides plenty of distance (i.e., second shot on par-5 holes)

- Swing at less than full speed on the forward swing

- Sweep the ball off the grass

- When the ball is settled down a bit in the first cut, use a three-quarter's swing (center ball position as noted above), and create a more descending blow

Strategy

- Know how to detect a flyer—for example: the ball is sitting up on the first cut of rough, sitting up in the primary rough with grass growing toward the target, half-covered by grass, or sitting in wet grass

- Decide if you can sweep the ball or if a steeper, more descending blow (as you would for a regular shot) is required. The ball must be sitting up nicely in the first cut (or sitting up in the primary rough) to sweep the ball; otherwise, if the ball is down and the lie somewhat protected, move the ball back to center to encourage a descending blow instead of a sweep

- Rehearse the shot, both physically and mentally before you execute

- Sometimes a flyer lie is great when you need extra distance

Swing Thoughts

- Smooth forward-swing tempo

- Level approach at impact when the ball is sitting up in the rough—sweep it

- Steeper approach when ball is sitting down—take a divot

BALL NESTLED DOWN IN PRIMARY ROUGH

Setup

- Use one or two more clubs than normal to account for decreased distance in thick grass (e.g., if the distance calls for a 7-iron, use a 6-iron or even a 5-iron for this shot)

- Grip down one inch for more control

- Stand one inch closer to the ball

- Firmer grip pressure in both hands

- Ball position in center of stance

- Align body and clubface to hit a fade: align body along line you want to start the ball

Swing

- Swing back along the line of your shoulders, but lift the club more with the arms

- Swing down along the line of your shoulders

- Maintain firm grip pressure through the shot to keep the clubface from closing

- "Cut" the ball out of the grass

- Let the club work down into the grass on the forward swing—take a divot

- Rotate through the shot into a full finish

Strategy

- Use this strategy when the ball is down in the primary rough, but not buried

- Even though you're set up to hit a fade, the ball won't curve as much from deep grass

- Rehearse the shot; imagine "cutting" the ball out of the long grass

Swing Thoughts

- Picture a more up-and-down shape to the swing

- Don't overswing wildly; concentrate on an aggressive pass and full finish to get through the grass

- Maintain grip pressure to prevent the clubface from closing

BALL BURIED IN DEEP ROUGH

Setup

- Use a lofted club for this shot—not more than an 8-iron

- Grip down two inches for more control

- Increase grip pressure in both hands

- Ball position back of center

- Set your hands slightly ahead of the ball

Swing

- You should feel as though you're lifting the club directly up and away from the ball on the backswing

- Little body rotation going back

- Approach the ball on the same steep angle as the backswing, allowing hands to lead

- Quiet or passive lower body on the forward swing

- Keep hands and wrists firm through the hitting area

- Finish will be low—about waist high or slightly higher

Strategy

- Realize that you're in recovery mode—set yourself up for the next shot

- You're trying to create a steep angle of approach to get the clubface on the ball

- Trust the setup and the club you've selected to get the ball out—stay relaxed

- Pick your landing area and rehearse the shot from a similar situation—do you have a forward swing?

- The shot will come out low and hot, traveling about half the total distance on the ground

- You're going for placement, not distance

Swing Thoughts

- Lift the club on the backswing

- Allow for a low finish

- Use a smooth, but aggressive, forward swing

- Club works down into the ground to pop the ball out

BALL ON HARDPAN

Setup

- Use one more club since you'll be hitting a partial shot (e.g., if the distance calls for a 7-iron, use a 6-iron for this shot)

- Hold the club at the end of the grip

- Ball position back one inch toward center of stance

Swing

- Three-quarters arm swing in the backswing

- Swing generated mostly by upper body with minimal lower-body coil

- Make a smooth transition into the forward swing—lead with the hands

- Strike the ball first, allowing the club to work down into the ground at impact

- Trust the loft of the club to get the ball airborne

Strategy

- Assess the situation: if the shot calls for a wedge, make the setup and swing adjustments to hit a bump-and-run shot (see chapter 2) to eliminate the bounce effect that hard ground can have

- Know how the ball reacts from hardpan—know the trajectory and spin characteristics that affect overall distance

- Learning to hit this shot will help you master correct ball-striking

Swing Thoughts

- "Nip" the ball off the hardpan—try not to "scoop" it with the hands and wrists

- Take a divot

- Swing with a smooth tempo in the backswing and forward swing

Practice Strategies

THE FLYER LIE

Golf is one of the few sports that is practiced on different grounds than it's played on. The flat, manicured surface of the range is great for training golf swing mechanics, but we all know that the lies we get on the golf course are far from perfect. Many golfers don't make time in their practice sessions to experience even the most common of the awkward lies faced on the golf course. In order to keep your anxiety level in check and your confidence high when faced with a challenging lie, make some time for the following drills.

Fundamental Drill

Use the setup and swing keys in this chapter to prepare for a flyer—a shot in which the ball is sitting up in the rough. To practice the flyer lie, use a 6- or a 5-iron and hit balls teed up at driver height. You'll see that the only way to make solid contact is to sweep the ball off the tee, approaching impact from a level angle that allows you to strike the ball in the center of the clubface.

If possible, take a few balls and move to the side of the practice range to create different flyer lies. Craft a shot where the ball is teed up in the rough or where the grass is wet, one where the ball is sitting down a little and one with the ball buried in the rough. Use different clubs with each of these lies to see how the club reacts out of rough, and the resulting direction, carry, roll and trajectory that each situation produces.

Competitive Drill

To perform your best you need to simulate the conditions of play when you practice, and that means practicing from all types of lies—deep grass, divots, hardpan and flyers. Instead of nudging each practice ball up on a nice tuft of grass, practice by scraping a few balls over and play them as the rules of golf would have us do . . . as it lies. Make a commitment to practice at least one imperfect lie during your practice session. For example, you may choose to work on divots at one practice and shots from the rough the next. Use the five-ball drill for the selected shot and hit three of five acceptable shots from the imperfect lie to a specific target. How well are you able to control distance and accuracy? The more you practice, the better you will get!

SIX

THE HANGING LIE

Because the World Isn't Flat

*"Start each hole with an awareness that there may
be subtle or mysterious elements waiting
to sabotage your game."*
—Robert Trent Jones, Jr.

Each spring, the best golfers in the world converge on Augusta National Golf Club for the Masters. If you're a golf fan, you're very familiar with the fast, undulating greens, the water hazards and the nerves that a Masters champion has to conquer. But unless you've ever attended the tournament in person, you have no idea how hilly the course is. Competitors are forced to play shots from uphill, downhill and sidehill lies on virtually every hole.

Sure, golf would be a much easier game if you could play every shot off of a flat lie. But since the world is round and covered with hills, valleys and mountains, it's unrealistic to expect much of a break from the effects of terrain when you're on the course. And you shouldn't. One of the great pleasures of golf is gaining the skills that let you handle all types of terrain.

Uneven lies require modifications to both the setup and the golf swing. A sloping lie changes launch conditions and affects the distance, direction and trajectory of the shot. But none of that will matter if you don't make solid contact. In this chapter you'll learn everything you need to know about the ups and downs you'll encounter on the golf course and how they affect your game.

FEATURED SHOT:
THE HANGING LIE—BALL BELOW YOUR FEET

No shot in golf is tougher than the hanging lie, where the ball is significantly below your feet at address. Even the touring professionals have trouble with this shot. Still, there's no reason you can't play this shot consistently well.

Visualizing the Shot

The first thing you need to know is how the ball is going to react. A good rule of thumb is that the ball tends to go in the direction of the slope. In this case, expect the ball to slide to the right.

Also, the slope of the ground effectively increases your spine tilt, which causes your swing plane to become more upright and vertical. The slope changes the effective lie angle, making it more flat. These factors combine to encourage a left-to-right shot.

The hanging lie is a tough one. You need to stand closer to the ball, with more bend in your knees. This shot tends to slide to the right. Aim accordingly.

The Setup

Start by using more club to account for the more vertical plane and the left-to-right shape that the hanging lie will generally produce. Hold the club at the very end of the handle. You'll need all the length you've got to swing down and through the ball.

Balance is the key to consistency from the hanging lie, so you need to pay extra attention to your stance. It's the foundation on which everything else is built. Widen your stance to shoulder width. A wider stance lowers your body's center of gravity to help you stay balanced throughout the swing and brings you down to the ball. Get even closer to the ball by increasing your knee flex. Your weight should be positioned on the balls of your feet.

Align the clubface along the line on which you want the ball to start, and then align your body along a line parallel left to the clubface. As for ball position, it should be just the same as for a normal shot.

The Swing

The most important factor in playing a good shot from a hanging lie is to hit the ball solidly. It's very easy to come out of this shot and top it. It's also easy to lose your balance and fall forward during the swing, hitting the ball on the hosel. The bottom line: If you try to get too much out of this shot, things can go from bad to worse in a hurry.

The slope of the hanging lie creates a more vertical backswing, as you can see here.

Maintain your knee flex throughout the swing—you need to stay down after this one.

I recommend using a three-quarters backswing for this shot. The arms and shoulders control the backswing, with very little lower-body rotation. By shortening the swing and letting the arms take control, you'll naturally eliminate a lot of unnecessary motion. It's absolutely essential that you stay down and through the shot. Focus on maintaining your knee flex throughout the entire swing. This will help you stay down. Make a nice, controlled swing, allowing the body to follow the arms on the forward swing.

Take a couple of practice swings before you hit the shot. Be sure to find an area where the slope is similar to the situation you'll have when you address the ball. Concentrate on tempo, rhythm, length of the swing and the bottom point, where the club hits the ground. Now you're ready to play.

By far the most important part of any shot is your familiarity with it. It's very difficult to play a shot you've never practiced. Incorporate the hanging lie into your practice sessions, especially if you plan to play on courses in hilly areas. As you get a feel for the tendencies of your shots from the hanging lie, experiment with factors such as club selection, swing length and pace, and clubface position at address. Some of my professional students, for instance, simply close the clubface slightly from a hanging lie and then align square to the target line rather than playing for a slight fade.

This is a difficult lie to master, but working on it brings a lot of benefits. Anyone who can consistently hit the ball well from a hanging lie is likely to be an overall good striker of the ball. With a little bit of effort, you won't feel as if you've been hung when you find the ball below your feet.

BALL ABOVE YOUR FEET

Most golfers feel much more comfortable when the ball is above their feet than they do when it is below. Don't be lulled to sleep, however. The ball above your feet can be a very troublesome lie because it sets you up to hit a "hot" shot that has the potential to fly or roll past your target and into trouble. So it's very important to know what

When the ball is above your feet, stand taller and grip down to compensate. This shot may fly to the left. Protect against it by aiming right.

adjustments to make prior to attempting the shot.

When you play a shot with the ball above your feet, the club will naturally swing more around your body, on a flatter plane. The result is that you'll tend to approach impact from the inside, closing the clubface down as you swing through the hitting area. A closed clubface decreases the effective loft of the club, causing the ball to fly lower than normal and work to the left. In general, you should be able to use one club less. Since the swing and impact position resulting from this lie create a lower, hotter shot, make sure you choose a club with enough loft.

Start by gripping down on the club between one and three inches. The more severe the slope, the more you should grip down on the club. Since the ball is above your feet, it is closer to your body than a shot from a flat lie. Gripping down accommodates the effect of the slope. Position the ball in your stance just as you would for a shot from a flat lie. Don't play it too far forward, or you run the risk of hitting the ground first.

Keep in mind that the ball being above your feet will create right-to-left spin. Align the clubface to the right, on the line on which you want the ball to start. Adjust your body alignment accordingly.

Some players actually open the clubface slightly at address to add a little bit of loft and to resist the tendency to pull the shot. Experiment with this to see if it works for you.

Set your weight in the middle of your feet and stand slightly taller. Now you're set up to play the shot.

When the ball is above your feet, it's best to "sweep" it, just as

A ball above your feet will result in a backswing that works more around your body.

Maintain your "tall" setup all the way through the shot.

though it were on a tee. Make a controlled, three-quarters backswing. A good image to use here is a baseball swing. Your upper body and lower body must remain level as you swing more around your body on a flatter plane. Solid contact will deliver plenty of power.

DOWNHILL LIE

Downhill lies are quite common on golf courses, since many architects enjoy designing holes that play down to their targets. A downhill shot from a flat lie is a fairly easy one, but when the fairway itself slopes down, things get a little trickier.

Applying your knowledge of how the slope affects the flight of the ball, you should be able to determine that a downhill lie decreases the loft of the club, resulting in a lower trajectory. Take this into account as you select your club.

Set up with your spine perpendicular to the slope and your shoulders parallel to the ground so that the club swings up the slope going back and down the slope coming through. Distribute about 60 percent of your weight on your left side and position the ball slightly back in your stance. These adjustments will give you the proper amount of upper-body tilt so that you work with the slope. The hill will make it more difficult to turn and pivot around your right leg on the backswing. Close your stance slightly to give your body a little more room.

You need the proper amount of body tilt so that you work with the slope. Set your shoulders parallel to the ground with 60 percent of your weight on the left and ball positioned slightly back.

While the slope will de-loft the club, it will also tend to produce a shot that moves from the left to the right, because your swing plane will be more vertical than usual, and swinging down along the slope tends to hinder the release of the hands.

The common mistake among most golfers is to try to help the ball up into the air. Instead, concentrate on hitting down and through the ball, following the slope of the hill. You're not trying to pick the ball off the hill but instead to strike the ball just before hitting the ground.

UPHILL LIE

An uphill lie adds loft to your shot and results in a higher trajectory and shorter carry. Take at least one club more than you would normally hit, possibly two. Set up with your spine perpendicular to the slope and your weight positioned slightly on the right side. This posi-

Set up to play an uphill shot by tilting your right shoulder until your shoulders are parallel to the slope. Play the ball forward.

tions your shoulders parallel to the ground and allows you to swing down the slope going back and up the slope going through.

Play the ball toward the front of your stance, opposite your left heel. Since your forward swing will be working against the slope of the hill, flare your left foot out about a quarter turn toward the target to encourage weight transfer. Because your weight will naturally lag a little bit, it's easy to let the arms get ahead of the body. The result is a pull, a shot that flies straight but slightly left of the target line. Align your clubface and body slightly to the right of the end target to compensate for the tendency to pull the shot.

During the forward swing, concentrate on swinging along the slope. Stay with the shot all the way into a good, high follow-through. It's okay to allow your weight to lag on the right side, but be sure you rotate your body all the way through to face the target.

SEEING THE WAY OUT OF BLIND SHOTS

Uneven lies aren't the only difficulties you'll find on hilly courses. Architects often take advantage of the terrain to challenge golfers with blind shots to fairways and greens. You can have uphill or downhill blind shots, but in both cases, you must remember that the effect is intended to be psychological. The actual shot usually has ample margin for error as long as you make reasonably solid contact and have good direction.

On uphill blind shots, the only real mistake is to leave the ball short. Make sure you add enough club to cover the uphill portion of the shot. If the target is well above the fairway, you'll need at least one extra club and possibly two. For shots played to a target below you, you'll need to back off a club or two.

After selecting the club, pick an intermediate target. This could be a divot, a twig or any distinct mark between three to five yards in front of you, on the intended line of the shot. The intermediate target allows you to commit to a line for the shot. And trust and commitment are what blind shots boil down to.

Blind shots are mental traps. Don't fall into them.

Chapter Summary

THE HANGING LIE—BALL BELOW YOUR FEET

Setup

- Use one more club (e.g., if the distance calls for a 6-iron, use a 5-iron for this shot)

- Hold the club at the end of the grip

- Widen stance to shoulder width

- Increase knee flex to get down to the ball

- Ball position same as normal shot

- Aim clubface where you want to start the ball (left of the end target)

- Align body along a line perpendicular to the clubface

Swing

- Three-quarters backswing and forward swing

- Arms and shoulders control the backswing—little body rotation

- Allow body to follow arms on the forward swing

- Balance is key!

- Maintain knee flex throughout the swing

Strategy

- The ball tends to go in the direction of the slope

- Setup and swing adjustments produce a left-to-right ball flight

- Don't try to get too much out of this shot

- Rehearse the shot from a similar part of the slope—pay attention to the low point of the swing, the tempo and length of swing that allows you to stay balanced

- Some players may prefer to close the clubface slightly and align squarely to the target line rather than play for a slight fade

Swing Thoughts

- Stay down with the shot

- Maintain knee flex on the forward swing

- Make solid contact

BALL ABOVE YOUR FEET

Setup

- Use one less club (e.g., if the distance calls for a 6-iron, use a 7-iron for this shot)

- Grip down on the club one to three inches, depending on the severity of the slope

- Gripping down requires you to stand closer to the ball

- Ball position same as normal shot

- Set weight in the middle of your feet and stand slightly taller

- Aim clubface where you want to start the ball (right of the end target)

- Align body along a line perpendicular to the clubface

Swing

- Controlled three-quarters backswing

- Upper body and lower body must remain level as you swing more around your body

- Sweep the ball as if it were on a tee

- Balance and solid contact will deliver plenty of power

- Low finish

Strategy

- The ball tends to go in the direction of the slope

- Setup and swing adjustments produce a shot that flies left

- Don't try to get too much out of this shot

- A ball position that's too far forward may cause you to hit behind the ball

- Rehearse the shot from a similar part of the slope—pay attention to the low point, the tempo and length of swing that allows you to stay balanced

- Some golfers may prefer to open the clubface slightly to add loft and resist the temptation to pull the shot to the left

Swing Thoughts

- Sweep the ball

- Baseball swing

- Stay tall; level shoulder-turn in both directions

- Low finish

DOWNHILL LIE

Setup

- Use at least one less club, depending on the severity of the downhill lie (e.g., if the distance calls for a 6-iron, use a 7-iron for this shot)

- Set your shoulders parallel to the slope

- Sixty percent of your weight on the left side

- Aim slightly left of the end target

- Drop your right foot back slightly

- Ball position slightly back of normal

Swing

- Swing the club up the slope going back and down the slope on the forward swing

- Dropping the right foot back gives arms room to swing and helps you to pivot around the right leg going back

- Resist the temptation to help the ball up in the air by swinging up at the ball

Strategy

- A downhill lie decreases the effective loft of the club you're using

- This shot becomes more difficult with a club that doesn't have much loft

• Plan for a low trajectory shot that will roll more than normal once it hits the ground

• The ball will start straight, then may cut a little to the right—more so with a less lofted club

• Rehearse the shot from a similar part of the slope—note the low point of the swing

Swing Thoughts

• Swing along the slope

• Swing down and through the shot—some golfers even take a step toward the target after hitting the ball

UPHILL LIE

Setup

• Use at least one more club, possibly two, depending on the amount of slope (e.g., if the distance calls for a 6-iron, use a 5- or even a 4-iron for this shot)

• Set your shoulders parallel to the slope

• Sixty percent of your weight on the right side

• Aim slightly right of the end target

• Flare your left foot open a quarter turn to encourage weight transfer

• Ball position opposite the left heel

Swing

• Swing the club down the slope going back and up the slope on the forward swing

- Stay with the shot all the way to a complete, high follow-through

- It's okay to allow weight to lag on the right side, but rotate body fully to the target at the finish

Strategy

- An uphill lie increases the effective loft of the club you're using

- Because the slope makes your weight lag behind the arm swing, play for a pulled left shot

- Plan for a high trajectory shot that won't roll much once it hits the ground

- Plan for a ball flight that will fly straight, then finish left

- Rehearse the shot from a similar part of the slope—note the low point of the swing

Swing Thoughts

- Swing along the slope

- Swing through to a high, complete finish

- Make a smooth transition to the forward swing and finish in balance

Practice Strategies

UNEVEN LIES

Course designers either use the mounds, swales or other topography provided by nature or they build them in to make their golf courses challenging and esthetically pleasing. That's the beauty of the game of golf: not only do you need to master the mechanics of the swing, but you need to know how you use your imagination, inventiveness and course management to get around the course in as few strokes as possible. You also need to know when to take your lumps and play the shot that puts you in the best position for the next one. If, for example, you have to hit a 3-wood from a severe slope to reach the green, a golfer who manages the course well would opt for the best layup position. Use the following drills to discover your capabilities so you can successfully weigh the risks and rewards when faced with uneven lies on the course.

Fundamental Drill

Since most good practice ranges are relatively flat, you'll really need to look for opportunities to practice uneven lies. Some of the best specialty shot practice is done on the course in the early evening when you have the place to yourself. However, there's no reason you can't practice the setup and swing fundamentals described in this chapter anywhere you can find sloping territory—even if you can't hit balls.

Competitive Drill

If you can find a place to practice hitting balls from uneven lies, you can use the five-ball drill to chart your progress. Use four clubs, from either the odd or even set, that represent short-, mid- and long-irons and woods. Hit from the four situations described in this chapter: ball below and above your feet, and downhill and uphill lies. Score at least three of five acceptable shots with each club before moving to the next situation. From your practice will come a knowledge of how you tend to hit the ball on each of the different lies. Notice how much you tend to curve the ball, the trajectory of each shot and how well you are able to control distance.

SEVEN

LAG PUTTING

And Other Steps on the Dance Floor

*"Yes, that's a new putter.
The last one didn't float very well."*
—Craig Stadler

Ben Hogan once said that putting should be an entirely different game. Well, it is. Nothing can get you hot under the collar like a day of good ball-striking followed by three-putting and missed birdie chances. But putting is also the area of greatest opportunity for most golfers. The stroke is simple and much more natural than the full swing. Think back to all the times you've set a new personal best on the course or to the last time you were the big winner in your regular game. No doubt, your putter made the difference.

When it comes to the stroke itself, putting really is "different strokes for different folks." All you have to do is stand off to the side of the putting green at a Tour event to see that there is no right way or wrong way about it. Billy Mayfair wins his share of tournaments and money with a highly unorthodox stroke. But the bottom line on putting is getting the ball into the hole. If you're doing that, you're doing it right.

FEATURED SHOT: THE LAG PUTT

The biggest step you can take toward better putting is to eliminate three-putts. Three-putts turn eagles into pars, birdies into bogeys and pars into double-bogeys. You can prevent most of them simply by paying more attention to your preparation on longer putts. I can't tell you how many players I see who beat themselves by failing to properly read their putts and by neglecting the basics of speed control. In this chapter, you are going to learn how to develop putting strategies that will help you eliminate three-putts and even make a few long putts.

Reading the Green

To be a good lag putter, you need to be able to read the green properly. This is a skill that anyone can learn, but it requires experience and good technique. If you don't know what you're looking for, you won't get the information you need.

There are a number of factors involved in reading the green. The speed of the putting surface, the slope of the green and the surrounding topography will all have an impact on the putt. Are the greens wet or dry? Soft or firm? What are the wind conditions? All of these factors will come into play if you are to make an accurate read.

The best putters start reading the green before they ever reach it. In other words, they pay close attention as they walk up to the putting surface. Use this wide focus to determine topography and the lay of the land surrounding the green. From the fairway, you will have a better perspective of the overall slope and contour. Does the land run off toward a drainage? Most architects design greens to drain to specific areas. An effective way to determine the slope and break of greens is to locate those drainage areas. Narrow your focus as you reach the green by studying the undulations of the green around the hole.

What Kind of Putter Are You?

Just as there are different types of ball-strikers, there are different types of putters as well. I divide golfers into two putting groups—"die" putters who like to have the ball drop slowly over the lip of the hole, and "speed" putters who generally like to hit the back of the cup. For examples of great die putters, look no further than Ben Crenshaw or Phil Mickelson. When they miss a putt, it seems to end up sitting right at the edge of the cup. Speed putters include Tom Watson—in his heyday he was probably the greatest speed putter ever—Tiger Woods and Nick Price. A speed putter's misses usually go a foot or even two feet beyond the hole. In most cases, swing style and putting styles mirror each other. The more aggressive hitters of the golf ball tend to be speed putters, where the smooth swingers are often die putters.

Knowing what type of putter you are is crucial not just to speed control, which I'll discuss later, but also to determining the line of the putt. A die putter will usually play more break. A speed putter will reduce the break by making a more aggressive run at the hole. Also, the more you know about your own tendencies, the more you can modify them. Speed putting is very risky on fast, downhill putts. Likewise, if the greens are grainy and slow, die putters will need to make adjustments to their style.

Great putters are able to change their styles depending on the circumstances. When you are putting on very fast greens or have a downhill putt, it is a great advantage to be able to become a die putter, even if it goes against your natural style. And if you are on slow or grainy greens, you had better be able to adopt a speed putter's mind-set if you are going to have any success. You will need both styles during almost every round, sometimes on a single green.

Determining the Line of the Putt—Triangulation

Once you know the lay of the land and your own putting tendencies, you can begin to determine the line of the putt. I recommend a process called triangulation. Basically, you view the putt from three sides of a triangle.

Start by positioning yourself behind the ball and identifying the low side of the putt, a crucial bit of information. For example, if you have a 20-foot uphill putt that breaks from right to left, the left side of the hole will be the low side. Walk along the low side of the putt, looking for imperfections along the line, including ball marks, spike marks and bare spots. Use your feet to help you determine the severity of the slope, and use your small paces to help you get a better feel for the distance of the putt.

The most accurate read of the line comes from directly behind the hole, looking back to your ball. This is a better place to read the putt from primarily because the ball will be traveling at its slowest around the hole. The slower the ball rolls, the greater the effect of the green. How will the ball be breaking when it reaches the hole? Imagine yourself pouring water on the green around the hole. Whichever way the water would run is the way the putt will break.

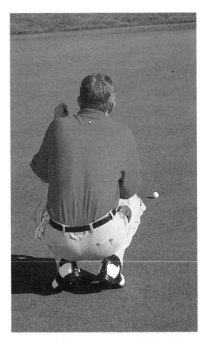

Now walk back to the low side of the putt, about halfway between the hole and your ball, several yards below the line of the putt. Why not look at the putt from the high side? You see more detail from

Reading the green from behind the ball helps you identify the low side of the putt, a crucial piece of information.

the low side. Think of looking up at a mountain from the bottom. You'll see much more detail of the mountain than you would if you looked down from the top. From the low side of the putt, the entire slope of the green is in front of you. You also get some great input on the distance of the putt from this angle. When you look right down the line of the putt, either from the ball or from the hole, it's difficult to judge the distance. Try looking straight down the shaft of your putter, from the butt of the grip to the head. Now hold the putter sideways in front of you. The length is much easier to gauge. The same is true with your putt.

Finally, read the putt from directly behind your ball. The primary goal here is to determine the starting direction of the putt. As you study the line, visualize the point at which the ball will begin to break back to the hole, and find an intermediate target between the ball and that point. The intermediate target will be useful as you align yourself for the stroke.

Reading the putt from the low side gives you great distance information.

Make sure you have factored the day's unique conditions into your read. Maybe there is early morning dew or rain on the green, which will slow down the putt and cause it to break less. Maybe it's hot and dry, and the greens are faster than normal. The key is to be aware of how conditions can affect the break of your putt.

One of the major mistakes I see golfers make is ignoring their read when aligning themselves to putt. Even though they have determined that the putt will break two feet to the left, they focus all of their alignment on the hole. Now is the time to use an intermediate target. Identify the spot where the ball will begin to work back to the hole and select a target between the ball and that point. This is the intermediate target. As you crouch behind the ball, keep the ball directly between you and the intermediate target. Only in the

Reading the putt from behind the hole will give you a better idea of how the ball will behave around the hole.

case of a dead-straight putt will that line go right to the hole. If you are overfocused on the hole, you will have trouble aligning yourself to the intermediate target, and that is the key to starting the ball on the proper line.

The Pre-Putt Routine

If you don't already have a regular pre-putt routine, you should work on developing one. There are two elements to the pre-putt routine—the mental and the physical. For the mental side, take your time reading the putt. Think like a champion as you prepare for the stroke. In other words, concentrate on what you want to do, not on what you don't want to do. I can't tell you how many times I've heard someone say after missing a putt, "The last thing I told myself was 'don't leave it short.'" Speak to yourself in positive terms, not negative ones.

Reading the green is part of both your mental and physical routine. Enter your routine as soon as you approach the green, when you begin reading the lay of the land with your wide focus. Mark and clean the ball to make sure it will roll properly. Then read the green, using the triangulation method. Pick the line and visualize the ball rolling, at actual speed, along the line until it drops into the hole.

You are now mentally prepared to make the stroke. Continue your physical routine as soon as you replace the ball on your mark. Many players line the ball up so that the brand logo points down the line of the putt. I like the idea of positioning the ball the same way every time. It's simply a good trigger for your mind.

Distance Control

Many golfers think putting is all about reading the break. But if you can't control the distance of your putts, then the best read in the world won't do a thing for you.

When I work with students on distance control, the first thing I do is pick up a golf ball, toss it to them, and have them toss it back to me. Then I ask them how they determined how far to throw it. Did they

No matter how long the putting stroke, it should be the same length back and through.

estimate the distance between the two of us? Did they take a couple of practice tosses to make sure they had it right? No, of course not. They looked, their minds calculated the proper distance, and then they tossed the ball, knowing that it would come right to me. This is the kind of distance control reflex that you should aspire to on the golf course. Your mind knows how to work with your muscles to produce the proper amount of force, as long as you stay relaxed and supply an adequate target.

Now take one or two practice strokes, rehearsing the length and pace of the stroke. The practice stroke length and pace should be the same as the actual putt. After your practice stroke, align yourself and prepare to make the stroke. Take one look at the hole and use your eyes to scan back from the hole to the ball. Within a second of returning your eyes to the ball, make the stroke. There's no point in making lag putting any more difficult than it already is.

Follow the Ball

Your first putt will tell you a lot about your upcoming second putt and can help you avoid costly three-putts. That's why you should never turn away from a putt that is rolling toward the hole. Instead, watch it closely. The last five feet of the putt will show you how the ball is going to behave around the hole. If your putt travels past the hole, you'll get to see exactly how the ball is going to break on your next putt. This is a great lesson and something that every good putter does. You may not be happy that you missed, but you'll be a lot happier knowing what the next putt is going to do than you will be if you have to start all over from scratch. You can also get valuable information by watching the behavior of your playing partner's putts.

Short Putts and Comebacks

There aren't any great secrets to holing short putts. If there were, someone would have discovered them by now, and no one would ever miss a three-footer. The key to these putts is alignment, tempo and, most of all, confidence. I encourage most golfers to take an aggressive approach to short putts. Imagine the ball hitting the back of the cup as it dives into the hole. It's when you try to get too cute with short putts that you find yourself in trouble.

In most cases, the read will be fairly simple. Only on the most severe slopes will you need to play the ball outside the hole. Find a spot on the back of the hole and drill it into your mind. It may be on the left or right side of the cup, depending on the break, but you want to play the short putts as straight as possible.

Make sure you are aligned properly, using the entire face of the putter. Both the heel and the toe should be square to the line of the putt. Now concentrate on making a rhythmic stroke, keeping your head and body still as you stroke the putter an equal distance back and through. Accelerate with your hands and the handle of the club as you stroke through the ball. Keep your eyes from looking ahead of the ball. A good image to keep in mind is to visualize a coin lying directly beneath your ball. You want to determine whether the coin is heads-up or tails-up before looking to see if you made the putt.

A Word on Putters

There are hundreds of different putters on the market today. Still, most fit into three different categories—mallet heads, blades and offset-style heads. Which one is right for you? Only you can answer that question. In earlier years, there was great variation in putting surfaces among courses, even courses in one region of the country. Golfers would have a heavy, mallet-head putter for slower greens and a lighter blade-style putter for faster greens. Today, advances in course maintenance and agronomy have eliminated many of those variations, making putter selection more of a matter of personal choice.

Putting is all about confidence. Most golfers I've known wouldn't hesitate to switch putters if they felt a change would make a difference. Paul Azinger won tournaments several years ago with a space-age putter called "the Thing." It was working for him. What can you say?

Regardless of the putter you use, you should know how to find its sweet spot. When you strike the ball on the sweet spot, you get a true roll and distance consistency. Hitting the ball on the heel or toe of the putter will cause the face to twist ever so slightly and will decrease your chances of making the putt. Find the sweet spot by holding the putter between your thumb and index finger at the end of the grip and tapping the face. Some putters have sweet spots toward the heel, others out toward the toe. Take a magic marker and make a small mark on the sweet spot and then make sure that's where you line up every time. Putts are just like all other shots—when you strike the ball on the right part of the clubface, the results are generally good.

RULES ON THE GREEN

While putting may be the "simple" part of playing golf, it can also be complicated from a rules perspective. Some of the best players in the world have lost tournaments by not knowing the rules that govern play on the putting green. Here are a few guidelines to help you stay on the right side of the law.

1. The fringe is not the green. You may mark your ball on the fringe if it interferes with another golfer's shot, but you cannot clean it, and you must replace it exactly as it was lying previously. Also, if your ball is on the fringe, you may not repair ball marks on the fringe until your ball is resting on the green.

2. The accidental stroke. In the 1997 Tournament Players Championship, Davis Love III was playing well and poised to pick up valuable Ryder Cup points. On the green of the devilish par-3 17th, however, he accidentally hit his ball with the toe of his putter while making a practice stroke. He assessed himself a two-shot penalty, marked the ball and then played from the new position. What he didn't know, however, was that the rules require you to replace the ball to its original position if you accidentally move it. The violation wasn't reported until after the

completion of his round, and since he had failed to assess himself another penalty for not replacing the ball, he was disqualified.

3. Mark these words. The most common rules infraction on the putting green is failure to replace a mark moved at the request of another golfer. Bruce Fleischer almost cost himself a victory on the Senior Tour during the 1999 season when, at the 18th hole (and with a four-shot lead), he moved his mark at the request of a fellow competitor. He forgot to move the mark back to its original position, playing instead from the spot he had moved it to. Fortunately, a spectator informed him of his violation before Fleischer signed his scorecard. Even with the two-shot penalty, he won by two.

Chapter Summary

LAG PUTTING

Reading Greens

- Start your read from the fairway using a wide focus—survey the topography locating mountains or bodies of water that dictate the general slope of the land

- Survey the slope and contour around the green for drainage areas

- Locate the break point by reading the putt from three vantage points: from behind the hole, from the low side and from behind the ball

Speed Control

- Note factors and conditions that influence speed, such as: uphill or downhill slope, type and length of grass, soft and wet or hard and dry ground

- Develop a stroke that produces consistent centerface contact

- Swing the putter an equal distance back and through with even rhythm

- Keep head and body still—the hands and putter handle lead the stroke

Strategy

- You need to learn how to effectively combine your read with the proper speed

- Know what kind of putter you are—speed putter or die putter

- Die putters play more break, speed putters play less break

- Adapt your style to fit the situation, e.g., speed putters need to adopt a die-putting style on fast downhill putts

- Your putting style often mirrors that of your full swing

- Be observant—watch your ball as it rolls by the hole to learn the break of your next putt, and observe the putts of your playing partners

- Don't overread short putts unless the slope is severe

Keys to Lag Putting

- Developing and using a consistent pre-putt routine is crucial to peak performance

- Always align the putter face to the break point (not the hole) on a breaking putt

- Commit to your read—don't second-guess yourself over the putt

- Trust your eyes to tell your muscles just how much energy is required to stroke the ball from point A to point B

Practice Strategies

LAG PUTTING

Because putting comprises roughly 40 percent of your score in a round of golf, being able to putt well is critical to reaching your scoring potential. If you consider how simple the mechanics of the putting stroke are to learn and master relative to the complexities of the full swing, it's easy to see that almost every golfer has the potential to become a single-digit handicapper in putting. All it takes is a little practice.

Fundamental Drill

Pick several breaking putts on the practice green and work to improve your accuracy and distance control by reading the green from the three angles described in this chapter and going through your pre-putt routine. Your goal is to improve your accuracy with each successive putt.

Competitve Drill

Use the safety zone drill described here to improve your distance control on long putts. Choose a hole on the practice putting green and pace off distances from the hole of 20, 30 and 40 feet. Putt three balls to the hole from each distance. Your goal is to make the putt, but if the ball misses it should be within the safety zone around hole. Your safety zone will depend upon your skill level. To start, make it the length of your putter. As you improve, make the zone the length of the grip or within the "leather" around the hole. Score points as follows: two points for a made putt, one point for a ball in the safety zone, and zero points for a ball that's outside the safety zone. There are 18 possible points in this game, but pick a target score to start and keep track to record your personal best. The next practice session, vary your distances from the previous session. For example, you may choose to move to 40, 50 and 60 feet.

Competitive Drill with a Friend

Play seven-up with a friend to practice competitively. This game is designed to sharpen your green reading, distance control and accuracy skills under gamelike conditions. You and a friend each have one ball. Whoever putts first chooses a putt from any distance to any hole on the practice green and you both take a turn at making the same putt. If you make the putt you score two points. If neither makes the putt, the person who putts the ball closest gets one point. If you three-putt you score a minus point. The first to seven points wins the game. What's good about this game is that it simulates the conditions you face on the golf course: You have one chance to perform, you're using your pre-putt routine for each putt and you're keeping score. You may even have a little wager riding on the outcome.

Preparing to Play

When you're warming up prior to a round of golf, I suggest you putt with only one ball. Choose a combination of long and short putts and knock in each putt. Using only one ball and performing your pre-putt routine for each putt, as you would on the course, gets your mind prepared for competition.

EIGHT

THE RUNNING CHIP

Scoring Around the Collar

"Give luck a chance to happen."
—Tom Kite

One of the greatest—and most annoying—things about golf is that every shot counts the same, whether it's a 300-yard drive or a tap-in putt. This equality places an emphasis on an effective short game. And nowhere is your short-game execution more critical than in chipping situations, where your ball is just off the green. Watch the professionals prepare for a chip shot on TV, and you'll often hear the announcer say, "He's trying to make this one." That's not an exaggeration.

Perhaps there's no more famous chip than the shot Larry Mize made on the 11th hole at Augusta National Golf Club for his playoff victory at the 1987 Masters. Augusta National, with its closely mowed fairways, is a great chipper's course. Few holes allow the lies necessary to hit a flop shot, and the greens are fast and undulating, favoring the player who can minimize air time and get the ball rolling as soon as possible. Mize's chip is a textbook example. He had missed the green to the right, leaving himself a slippery, right-to-left breaking shot. Had he chosen to pitch the ball in the air, he would have had to hit the perfect shot simply to keep the ball on the green. Instead, he chipped the ball so that it landed just short of the green and rolled smoothly as a putt all the way into the hole. Ironically, the golfer Mize beat in that playoff—Greg Norman—has a wonderful chipping game and once defeated Paul Azinger in a playoff at Doral by holing a chip shot for an eagle on the first playoff hole. The moral of these stories is that a good chipper is never out of the hole or the tournament.

Chipping, next to putting, is the simplest stroke in golf. Anyone can become a good chipper. In this chapter I'll show you the fundamentals of club selection, the basic chipping stroke, advanced chipping and specialty shots around the collar, and how you can turn some of your missed greens into birdie chances.

FEATURED SHOT: THE RUNNING CHIP

One of the questions I hear from many golfers is, "When does chipping end and pitching begin?" As a rule, you can play chip shots from just off the putting surface to about 15 or 20 feet from the surface. If you need to carry the ball much farther than that, you will need to use a bigger swing and more of a pitching technique. The chip is designed for minimum air time and maximum ground time. The idea is to get the ball onto the green as soon as possible and let it roll to the hole. The landing area for most chip shots is about three feet beyond the edge of

Regardless of the overall length of the chip, the landing area stays the same.

the fringe. This takes the fringe out of play, decreasing the chance of an unpredictable bounce.

There are two reasons why you should use this type of shot whenever you can. First, it's easier to hit a target closer to you than one that is farther away. Stand several paces away from the practice green and chip balls into an imaginary three-foot circle just a yard beyond the fringe. Now move the imaginary circle about ten yards beyond the fringe. Which shot is easier to hit?

The second reason is that the ball holds its line better on the ground. The higher and farther a ball flies, the more unpredictable it is when it lands. It could check up too quickly, release and travel too far, or hit an imperfection on the green and bounce off-line. A well-executed chip shot rolls almost like a putt and is very predictable and repeatable.

Club Selection—the Ratio System

When it comes to chipping, there are two schools of thought about club selection. The first is to use the same club for chips of all lengths. There have been great chippers who followed this philosophy, but I believe that most golfers perform better when they vary their club selection according to the shot, keeping the stroke and landing area constant. When you use only one club, you must compensate for distances and terrain by opening or closing the clubface or somehow changing the stroke. Worse yet, the landing area changes from shot to shot. This decreases your consistency and takes away from the simplicity of the shot.

So, how do you select the proper club for a given chip? You should use everything from a sand wedge to a 5-iron, depending on the length of the shot. First, you need to realize that there are two distance factors involved in chipping: the distance from the ball to the landing area—three feet onto the green—and the distance from the landing area to the hole. To pinpoint club selection, you can use a simple mathematical formula that serves as an excellent reference point. Here is the carry-to-roll ratio for the chipping clubs:

Club	Carry : Roll Ratio
SW	1 : 1
PW	1 : 2
9-iron	1 : 3
8-iron	1 : 4
7-iron	1 : 5
6-iron	1 : 6
5-iron	1 : 7

This may seem complicated at first glance, but it's actually very simple. Remember, you are going to use the same landing area with each club. Pace off the distance from your ball to the landing area. For this example, say it's three paces. Then pace off the distance from the landing area to the hole. Let's say you've counted off 12 paces from the landing area to the hole. So the carry-to-roll ratio would be 3 (paces from the ball to the landing area) to 12 (paces from the landing area to the hole). The calculation 3:12 reduces to 1:4. So you would generally need an 8-iron for the shot.

Use these ratios as reference points. Chipping is not an exact science. You'll need to make adjustments for the lie of the ball, special conditions and your personal style. For uphill shots or extremely slow greens you may use a less-lofted club than the ratio indicates. For downhill shots or very fast greens, a club with more loft. But these references can certainly help in your club selection process. Develop a feel for the carry-to-roll ratio of different clubs by first estimating the distances and then by practicing and pacing off the actual distances you get from each club. Make notes and modify the carry-to-roll table to reflect your own chipping tendencies. By doing this, you'll sharpen your skills and become more accurate in choosing the proper club.

Preparing for the Shot

Prior to selecting your club, you should devise your strategy for the shot. Assess the lie of the ball. A ball sitting down in the grass, for instance, will tend to come out a little hotter than a ball sitting up. Evaluate the landing area—what will the ball do when it hits the green? Look at the carry-and-roll distances and the slope and speed of the green. Since chipping is much like putting, your preshot routine should closely resemble your routine for a putt. If any questions remain about the distance you must cover, look at the shot from the side for a better perspective. This provides better depth perception than a straight-down-the-barrel view. Read the green from the low side and pick a target that allows for the break of the shot. Now you're ready to select your club.

Once you have selected the club, take one or two practice strokes. The amount of energy required for a chip shot is about the same as for a putt of comparable length. As you take your practice strokes, rehearse the length and pace of the upcoming shot.

You should also determine whether to leave the pin in or out as you chip. I generally prefer to leave the pin in. If the ball is traveling too fast, like it is in most downhill chips or on very fast greens, the pin could be a great asset. If the ball is traveling slowly enough to fall into the hole on its own, the pin shouldn't be in the way. Some golfers say that they take the pin out if they're trying to hole the shot. If you feel that having the pin out helps you zero in on the target, then the mental edge you gain may outweigh any physical disadvantage of not having the pin to serve as a backstop. Be sure to check to see if the pin is leaning in the cup and remove it if it is.

The Chipping Stroke

Chipping is a stroke, not a swing. Step into position for a chip shot as if you were stepping into any other shot. First, align the clubface to the target. Use your regular grip. Grip down on the club you've selected until you have shortened it to the length of a putter. This means that every club will be effectively the same length. Stand closer to the ball so that the clubshaft is more vertical, allowing the clubhead to work up and down during the stroke. Bend from the hips and let your arms hang directly beneath your shoulders. Your eyes should be positioned just inside the target line. Align your shoulders parallel to the target line, since they will dictate the path of the stroke. Your feet should be close together to inhibit lower-body motion. The proper stance is slightly open, allowing freedom for the arms to swing. Play the ball a little right of center to encourage a slightly descending blow and set the majority of your weight on the left side. Use a slightly lighter than normal grip pressure for added touch, and set your hands just ahead of the ball, toward the front pocket of your pants.

Now make a one-lever motion. Perform the chipping stroke with your arms and shoulders, keeping your lower body still. The stroke is

*Set up for the running chip by
gripping down and standing closer
to the ball so that the shaft is almost
vertical. This allows the clubhead to
work up and down through the
ball. Position weight on the left side,
the ball back with hands set ahead
of the ball. Make a one-lever stroke
with a low follow-through.*

the same length back and through, with an even rhythm. Take the club straight back with minimal wrist break. With the ball back in your stance, and your hands and weight forward, the club will work up and descend into the ball, creating crisp contact. Lead with the handle of the club and finish with the clubhead low to the ground. This should be just enough to get the ball onto the green and headed toward the hole.

Advanced Chipping

Sometimes you find yourself in situations that require you to modify the basic chipping stroke. For instance, the ball may be sitting down slightly in the rough, just beyond the collar. In this case, you'll need to get a little more loft on the shot to carry the collar. Drop down a club. If the ratio system suggests an 8-iron, try a 9-iron instead. Then play the ball another inch farther right in your stance to make sure you hit the shot with a descending blow. This adjustment will de-loft the club, turning the 9-iron into an 8-iron. Likewise, if the ball is sitting up, you might want to position it in the center of your stance to encourage cleaner contact with a shallower stroke.

The "Pop" Shot

The best chippers have great imagination. Say your ball winds up in a relatively thick collar just a few feet from the green. The green is sloping away from you, meaning the ball will run quickly when it lands. You can't play a standard chipping stroke because you need to be more aggressive to get the ball out of the grass.

In case you haven't recognized it, this is precisely the situation Tom Watson had on the 71st hole of the 1982 U.S. Open. On top of the difficulty of the shot, he had Jack Nicklaus just a single shot behind him. Watson chose a sand wedge, knowing that all he had to do was fly the ball to the putting surface. He gripped down on the handle of the club, opened up the face to get the loft he needed and took an open stance with the ball positioned in the center. This shot requires a more

To hit the "pop" shot, break your wrists more sharply to create a more descending blow.

descending blow than a normal chip shot, meaning he had to break his wrists a little more on the backswing. Still keeping his lower body very quiet, he swung back along the line of his shoulders and then down and into the ball, letting the ground effectively stop the clubhead on the forward swing. The ball popped up, landed just on the putting surface and rolled straight toward the hole, tapped the pin and fell in for a birdie. Watson went on to win his only U.S. Open title.

That shot shows you all you need to know about advanced chipping. You won't be able to use the ratio system when you need to carry the ball the majority of the way to hole. Instead, experiment with the loft of the clubface, the position of the ball and the position of your hands at address. Keep the follow-through short and low to the ground at all times. In these cases, stick with your sand wedge and learn how the various setup and swing adjustments will affect the shot. Being able to improvise a simple shot for a tough situation is what great imagination on the golf course is all about.

Vary the carry of the shot by experimenting with the loft of the clubface, the position of the ball and the position of your hands at address.

Against the Collar

As course conditioning has improved over the years, more and more courses now encircle the greens with a collar of thick grass. Sometimes you'll find your ball nestled up against the collar, making a conventional chip shot almost impossible. In the past, golfers would try to overcome this situation by using a bellied wedge, or by making a chipping stroke with the intent of hitting the ball with the leading edge of the wedge. This isn't a bad shot, but there's virtually no room for error. Instead, you should turn to a shot that you've no doubt seen on television over the past few years—the utility wood chip. Utility woods have a nice flat sole and a lot of mass to help ensure solid contact. Don't worry if your friends and playing partners accuse you of showing off when you pull out the wood. This is a simple and effective golf shot, and those are the best kind.

Grip down on the club all the way to the end of the grip, so that your

A utility wood can be a great tool when you're against the collar. Play the ball back, gripping down to the shaft with your right hand, and then make a putting stroke, letting the clubhead work down into the ball.

right hand is actually on the shaft. Now stand closer to the ball so that the shaft of the club is nearly vertical. You don't need any hand action for this shot. Play the ball one inch back of center and position the hands slightly ahead.

Because of the position of the shaft, the clubhead will work more up and down than it would in a traditional chipping stroke. Stoke back and through the same length and pace, with your hand and the club's handle leading the head through impact. The shot should come out just fine, rolling from the start.

Don't Mess with the Texas Wedge

Golfers use the term "Texas Wedge" to refer to a putt from well off of the putting surface. Naturally, the shot originated in Texas, where sun and wind left the fairways hard and fast. I like a shot that rolls along the ground when you're playing from a tightly mowed area with no collar or other inconsistency to carry between your ball and the green. But once again, use a 3-wood or a utility wood rather than attempting this shot with a putter. A wood gives you a lot of mass behind the ball. And the 13 or more degrees of loft you have with a wood, compared to the 4 degrees you have with a putter, means you'll get the ball started consistently because it will have some slight lift off the clubface.

Use the standard chipping setup but position the ball just to the left of the center of your stance. Be sure to lead with your hands as you stroke through the ball, again using a one-lever stroke of equal distance and pace back and through.

When you hit the ball, it will go a few feet in the air and then land with enough overspin to carry the ball toward the hole. Experiment with this shot to see how comfortable you are. I think you'll be surprised.

Chapter Summary

THE RUNNING CHIP

Setup

- Use a regular, full-swing grip and align clubface squarely to the target

- Lighter grip pressure

- Grip down to the top of the shaft to shorten the club to putter length

- Stand closer so eyes are just inside the target line

- Keep your feet close together and take a slightly open stance

- Align shoulders parallel left of the target line

- Ball position back, opposite the instep of your right foot

- Hands positioned ahead of ball

- Majority of your weight on the left side

- For club selection: divide distance from the ball to the hole into a carry-to-roll ratio and use the chart on page 117 as a general guideline

Swing

- One-lever stroke with the arms and shoulders, keeping lower body still

- Stroke is the same length and pace, back and through

- Because the shaft is vertical like a putter, the path is straight back and through—not around the body, which can cause "fat" chips

- Let the club work up a little going back so it can return to the ball with a descending blow, creating crisp, ball-turf contact

- Avoid trying to lift the ball with the forward stroke

- Lead with the handle on the forward swing, keeping the clubhead low at the finish

Strategy

- A chip is designed to produce minimum air time and maximum ground time

- For greater control you want to get the ball on the ground and rolling as quickly as possible

- Approach a chip like a long putt—read the green, pick your landing area, rehearse the stroke and try to chip the ball so that it rolls close to or into the hole

- Landing area for most chips is three feet (or one stride) onto the green

- The landing area changes only if you can't land the ball onto a relatively flat surface

- The landing area and stroke remain constant—the club (and different amounts of loft) is the variable. Less loft equals more roll, more loft equals less roll

- Adapt the chipping ratio to suit the situation and your personal style—e.g., an uphill chip with wet grass may require a less lofted club than the chipping ratio suggests

Swing Thoughts

- Ball back, hands forward, weight forward

- Let the club work down into the grass on the forward swing

Practice Strategies

CHIPPING

The practice chipping green is a great way to familiarize yourself not only with the mechanics of the chipping stroke itself, but with the club selection method and the carry-to-roll ratio in this chapter. You can practice pacing off the carry distance from your ball to your landing area (always three feet onto the green) and the roll distance from the landing area to the hole. Reduce the paces to a carry-to-roll ratio and check the chart. With a little practice, you'll become familiar with what a 1:4 carry-to-roll ratio looks like, for example. You can test your skills at eyeballing the carry-to-roll ratio from the side, then pacing it off to gain confidence in your decision making. You want to become familiar with this approach during practice so that when you get to the course, you have a strategy to execute a successful chip, while still keeping pace of play.

Fundamental Drill

Go to the practice chipping green and place a tee or coin to identify your landing area about three feet or one stride onto the putting surface. Go through your bag, hitting your even clubs the first day and your odd clubs the next time. Hit five chips with each club with a focus on hitting crisp, solid chips that land near the tee or coin. Concentrate on keeping the same tempo and length of swing on the backswing and the forward swing. As you're developing a consistent chipping stroke, notice how far the ball rolls after it hits your target landing area. You'll be able to start tailoring the carry-to-roll chart provided in this chapter to your own chipping style. Finish by choosing a few chips that are a little more uphill, downhill or sidehill to see how the terrain affects your ability to execute a chip with the right distance.

Competitive Drill

The five-ball drill is an excellent way to improve your chipping. Choose a chip shot around the practice green. Select a club for the shot and pull over five balls. Your goal is to chip balls within a clublength of the hole to score points before you can choose to chip to another target. There are three scoring levels for this game: level 1, beginners should strive for three of five balls within a clublength; level 2, intermediate players should try for four of five; and level 3, advanced/pro-level players must get five of five within a clublength. You can make it even more challenging by making the target within the leather. You get three attempts to score three points out of five balls. If you should chip a ball in the hole, it counts for two points. Only when you've scored three points can you choose another target or move to another exercise.

NINE

THE STANDARD PITCH

Stocking Your Game's Bullpen

"Heartaches usually begin when your're 50–75 yards out from the green. That is the vale of tears."

—Tony Lema

If you asked amateur golfers to name the biggest difference between their games and a tour pro's game, most of the answers would revolve around ball-striking. True, tour professionals tend to hit the ball longer and straighter, but in my mind the biggest difference is wedge play. Think of the manager of a baseball team. When the game is on the line, he'll turn to his bullpen, bringing in pitchers with specific characteristics to face certain hitters. If a hitter tends to hit ground balls, you want a pitcher who keeps the ball down. Your wedge play is the bullpen of your golf game.

When an outstanding player gets within 100 yards of the green, he is in the "scoring zone." More importantly, he's working with the most creative part of his game. Unlike most amateurs, a tour pro doesn't look at the shot as simply a wedge shot. Instead, he looks at all the factors that could influence the shot—distance, lie, pin position, shape and contour of the green, wind—and then determines what type of shot will afford him the best chance of getting close to the hole.

Distance control with wedges starts by understanding how to alter your setup, arm swing, body pivot and the clubface to produce a shot that flies low, at standard height or high depending on what you need at the time. For instance, if you're playing a 60-yard shot into the wind or if the green slopes from back to front and the pin is back, you will probably want to play a shot that flies lower and rolls a little more once it hits the ground. In still conditions, with an accessible pin, you'll likely play a standard shot from that same position, making as few adjustments as necessary to hit a solid medium-trajectory shot to the target. Finally, if you need to get the ball into a tight space and stop it quickly, you'll have to be able to bring that 60-yard pitch in high and soft.

DIAL UP THE DISTANCE

Distance control is crucial to good wedge play, but distance control is impossible if you don't have a good feel for distances. Time and time again players come to me with what they think are distance-control problems when in fact they have distance-judging problems. Here's a typical scenario. A golfer has been on the range, practicing what he thinks are 60-yard wedge shots. Then he gets out on the course, finds a yardage marker that indicates he has a 60-yard shot and executes the same swing he has been using on the practice tee. The ball sails 10 yards over the green.

The problem here is that he was never practicing a 60-yard shot in

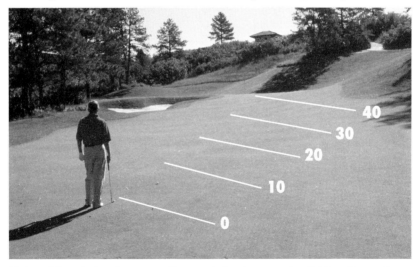

Being able to judge the correct distance is key to accurate pitching. It may be helpful to break distances up into increments with visual references.

the first place. Here are some guidelines for learning to judge distances more accurately.

- Always practice to a specific target.

- Be aware of the yardage markers on the range.

- If your practice facility offers a distance-finding system, such as the Bushnell system, use it. Most range finders will return very accurate yardages to marked pins. They can be very helpful in familiarizing yourself with distances.

- Pace halfway to your target and multiply the result by two.

- Break distances up into increments with visual references. I usually think of distances by visualizing a marked football field. I know about how far ten yards is, so I can look at a distance and apply ten-yard markings to it in my mind, yielding up a pretty accurate result.

FEATURED SHOT: THE STANDARD WEDGE SHOT

Almost all golfers feel more comfortable hitting a full shot than taking a half or three-quarters swing. That's because you've conditioned yourself to the timing and feel of a full swing. But more than 60 percent of all shots in a round of golf travel only 100 yards or less. This means that you have to be able to control the distance of your wedge shots or risk adding costly strokes to your scores.

In this chapter, we're going to look at three different wedge shots and give you the information you need to be able to play them from just about any distance, but here we'll start with the standard wedge shot. Under normal conditions, this is your go-to shot from 100 yards in, and it will serve as an excellent reference model when we turn our attention to varying the trajectory of your approaches.

For most partial wedge shots, you should use your sand wedge instead of your pitching wedge. The added loft of the sand wedge produces a shot that flies higher with more backspin, allowing you to be more aggressive with the shot.

For a standard pitch, set up with your hands even with the ball and weight evenly distributed between left and right. Swing the club the same length on the backswing and forward swing.

Grip down on the club about an inch for greater control and stand about an inch closer to the ball. Finally, narrow your stance so that it's just slightly wider than your hips. These adjustments will allow you to have the freedom of movement you'll need to swing rhythmically, regardless of the distance of the shot.

For a standard wedge shot, play the ball about an inch left of the center of your stance. Set up with your hands in a neutral position, so they are even with the ball. This will help you create an impact position in which the handle of the club and the clubhead arrive at the ball at the same time. Distribute your weight evenly between your left and right sides and set your upper body directly on top of your lower body.

The key to this shot is to swing the club the same length on the backswing and forward swing. It's just a miniature version of the full swing. The mistake I most often see amateur golfers make when they attempt a standard wedge shot is that they take the club back too far and then quit on the shot, failing to make an aggressive pass at the ball. To prevent deceleration and quitting on the shot, be sure that you allow your body to pivot with the arms on the forward swing. Again, your pivot should correspond to the length of the arm swing, ending with a finish that has your weight on the left side and your belt buckle pointing at the target.

TAKING THE LOW ROAD

Far too many golfers think they can only hit higher shots with wedges. If you go out on the practice tee at a Tour event, you'll see plenty of low wedge shots. Paul Azinger is a true master of the low sand-wedge shot that flies in hot, skips once or twice on the green and then spins to a quick stop. This is a shot you'll love having in your bag when conditions are windy or when the pin is on the back half of a green.

The key phrase I tell my students when working with them on low wedge shots is, "A low shot requires a low finish." What I mean by that is that you want to swing into impact with some acceleration but resist the tendency to swing into a full, high follow-through. Far too often, you'll end up scooping the ball with your wrists and hitting it much higher than you intended.

For lower pitches, set your hands ahead and play the ball farther back in your stance. The backswing is longer than the forward swing. Finish with your body facing the target, with the hands and club in a low position.

You might ask why you shouldn't just drop down to a pitching wedge when you want to hit it lower. Sometimes that's a good strategy if you need added distance and a lower trajectory under special conditions such as wind or to reach the pin cut back on a very deep green. But my goal here is to teach you how produce any trajectory simply by making setup and swing adjustments. Also, your sand wedge is shorter than the pitching wedge, delivering more directional control. And the psychological advantage of knowing you've got your scoring club in your hand is extremely valuable. Take a look at some of the time-worn wedges in PGA Tour players' bags, and you'll know what I mean.

To set up for this shot, move the ball back about one inch from the center of your stance. Now set your hands forward so that your hands and the club's handle are actually ahead of the ball. By placing your hands in this position, you hood the clubface slightly, de-lofting it to produce a lower shot. It's crucial to maintain this position through impact so that you keep the clubface de-lofted. Set your shoulders nearly parallel to the ground. This encourages you to stay level throughout the shot and ensures you won't get too far behind the ball at impact.

To hit a solid low wedge shot, your backswing should be longer than your follow-through. Remember that you've set up to de-loft the club, so if you use the same swing speed and length as you did for the standard wedge shot, the ball will fly a little farther and higher. The key element to the low wedge shot is to use a shorter arm swing, particularly on the follow-through. Make sure you allow your body to pivot to face the target as you swing through the hitting area. By pivoting with your body, you'll be able to keep your hands in front of the clubhead, maintaining the slightly hooded clubface position. With a good pivot through impact, you'll also have no reason to scoop the ball.

Finally, stay tall and level through the hitting area, finishing with good arm extension and the clubhead in a low position, matching the shot's low trajectory.

THE HIGH ROAD

We all have to hit the ball high from time to time. Maybe you're playing a shot to a pin tucked between two bunkers, or you need to clear some tree limbs that hang between you and the green. The high wedge shot can be a good friend to have in these situations, and based on what you already know about wedge play, it's not very difficult to play.

Start by opening the clubface slightly. An open clubface will cause the ball to fly to the right, so open your entire body a corresponding amount.

Play this shot with the ball one or two inches forward from the center of your stance and with your hands in a neutral position, or even slightly behind the ball. Tilt your spine to the right, lowering your right shoulder to distribute more of the weight to the right side at the address position. This will allow you to work more under the ball on the forward swing.

The swing for the high, soft wedge shot features a follow-through that is longer than the backswing. In other words, if you take a three-quarters backswing, you'll want to swing all the way into a full finish. Just as the low shot requires a low finish, the high shot requires a full, high finish. Programming this finish position into your mind helps you stay behind the ball with your body, adding loft to the club to produce the high trajectory.

As you swing, concentrate on keeping your upper body behind the ball. Again, you'll encourage a nice release and a slight "reverse C" finish position, which lets you take full advantage of the loft of the club.

ADVANCED DISTANCE CONTROL

In this chapter we've already discussed how to accurately judge distances and how to control the trajectory of your wedge shots. If you master those points, you'll go a long way toward improving your wedge play. But to break through from being a good wedge player to being a great wedge player, you need to understand not only the effects of clubface position—square, hooded or open—but also how to control the distance of your shots by managing the length and pace of the swing.

For high, soft pitches, play the ball slightly forward with hands in a neutral position—or even set slightly behind the ball. The forward swing will be longer than the backswing. The high shot requires a full high finish.

To gain better distance control, match the length and pace of the swing to the distance. For a standard pitch, always swing the club the same length back and through.

Length of Swing

Managing the length of your swing is especially important with your wedges. One of the most common flaws I see when high-handicappers get within 100 yards of the green is that they will use the same length swing. This means they have to slow the clubhead down with their body and hands on the forward swing, making it very easy to flinch and either skull the shot or hit it fat and leave it far short of the target.

The rules are simple: The shorter the shot, the shorter the swing; the longer the shot, the longer the follow-through. Always match your body pivot to the length of the swing. That's the only way you'll develop the sense of rhythm you need to produce consistent shots that fly the proper distances.

Pace of Swing

Here's another simple rule: The shorter the shot, the slower the swing. Your arms, club and body must move at a speed that matches the requirements of the shot. For a 70-yard pitch, that will be a faster speed than for a 40-yard pitch.

The next time you're on the range, try to hit a few shots with each of three swings—a full swing, a three-quarters swing and a half swing. Hit five balls with each swing at regular pace. Then try speeding up each swing length for five balls and slowing down each swing length for five balls. Concentrate on hitting the ball solidly, swinging with good rhythm and timing at every speed.

Once you know the adjustments to make for good trajectory control and distance control, you'll find yourself saving more pars, making more birdies and shooting lower scores, even when your ball-striking is less than perfect.

VISUALIZING TRAJECTORY

The greatest weapon you have on the golf course is the space between your ears. Your mind judges distance and directs muscle movement to produce the desired shot.

Develop greater mental and perception skills by visualizing as you practice. Imagine yourself playing shots to different targets and different pin positions. Try low shots that skip to the back of the green and high shots that stop quickly on a front tier. And everything in between.

Your mind will help instruct your body to make the proper adjustments. Combined with the shotmaking knowledge you have on controlling trajectory, this mental assist can be significant.

One green can offer different targets that require very different pitch shots.

BUILDING YOUR OWN WEDGE SYSTEM

Until about ten years ago, equipping your bag with wedges was pretty simple—you got a pitching wedge with your set of irons and selected a sand wedge you liked (for more information on sand wedges, see chapter 11). Today, there are literally hundreds of wedges to choose from. Pitching wedges, gap wedges, sand wedges with varying degrees of loft and bounce, and lob wedges all have their uses on the golf course.

Lob wedges with lofts of 60 degrees or more have become standard on the PGA Tour, although recently several players have stopped carrying them, feeling they didn't use the added loft enough to justify removing another club.

I recommend that you begin keeping track of how and how much you use each of your wedges. If you are constantly hitting partial shots with one of your wedges, then perhaps you need another one with a different amount of loft. Maybe you got a lob wedge thinking that it would help you greatly around the greens but have now found that you do better by simply manipulating the clubface of your sand wedge. In that case, you might do well to take the lob wedge out and make use of another fairway wood, utility wood or long iron.

Remember, it's what you do with the wedge that matters. What you want is a selection of wedges that gives you confidence from 100 yards in. If you've got that, then you've already got the right tools.

Chapter Summary

STANDARD WEDGE SHOT

Setup

- For most partial wedge shots (pitch shots), use your sand wedge. It has more loft than a pitching wedge so the ball will fly higher, straighter and with more backspin

- Grip down one inch

- Stand one inch closer to the ball

- Narrow your stance to just slightly wider than hips

- Ball position one inch left of center

- Hands in a neutral position, about even with the ball

- Distribute weight evenly left and right

- Set upper body directly on top of lower body

Swing

- The backswing and forward swing are of equal length—the length back and through being appropriate for the distance you want to carry the ball

- The pace of the swing is equal both back and through (slower for short shots, faster for longer shots)

- Don't quit on the shot—allow your body to pivot with the arms on the forward swing

- Allow the clubhead to work down into the ground on the forward swing—take a little divot

- Finish with your weight on the left side and your belt buckle pointing at the target

- Your wedge has plenty of loft to get the ball in the air—resist any temptation to scoop the ball with the hands and wrists

Strategy

- Assess the situation—for example, a standard wedge shot with normal trajectory should be used in still conditions to an accessible pin. Under normal conditions, this is your go-to shot from 100 yards and in

- Know the yardage for every wedge or pitch shot!

- Know how far the ball rolls once it hits the green

- Know the clubface position you're trying to produce at impact

- Visualize and rehearse the shot

Swing Thoughts

- Same length backswing and forward swing

- Swing with a smooth tempo on the backswing and forward swing

- Allow body to rotate to the target on the forward swing

LOW WEDGE SHOT

Setup

- Use sand wedge for this shot

- Grip down one inch, stand one inch closer to the ball

- Narrow stance to just slightly wider than hips

- Ball position one inch back of center

- Set hands and club handle ahead of the ball—this effectively de-lofts the clubface to produce a lower shot

- Set your shoulders nearly parallel to the ground

Swing

- The forward swing should be shorter and lower than the backswing

- The hands should lead the clubhead through the hitting area

- Allow your body to pivot to face the target on the forward swing

- Stay tall and level through the hitting area, finishing with good arm extension and the hands, arms and golf club in a low position

Strategy

- This wedge shot flies lower, farther and rolls more than the standard wedge shot

- Situations which require a low wedge shot: hitting into the wind, pin placement in back of the green, green slopes from back to front

- Know the flight-to-roll ratio of the low wedge shot to choose an appropriate landing area on the green

- Know the clubface position you're trying to produce at impact

- Visualize and rehearse the shot

Swing Thoughts

- A low shot requires a low finish

- Keep the hands in front of the clubhead to maintain a slightly hooded clubface position

- Swing with a smooth tempo on the backswing and forward swing

HIGH WEDGE SHOT

Setup

- Use sand wedge for this shot

- Open the clubface slightly and open entire body a corresponding amount

- Grip down one inch, stand one inch closer to the ball

- Narrow your stance to just slightly wider than hips

- Ball position one to two inches forward of center

- Set hands and club handle neutral to slightly behind the ball—this effectively adds loft to the clubface to produce a higher shot

- Tilt spine to the right, lowering the right shoulder to distribute more weight to the right side at address

Swing

- The forward swing should be longer and higher than the backswing

- Concentrate on keeping your upper body behind the ball

- Allow your body to pivot to face the target on the forward swing— clubs swings into a nice high position

Strategy

- This wedge shot flies higher, shorter and rolls less than the standard pitch

- Situations that require a high wedge shot: pin placement in front of the green just over a hazard, pin tucked between two bunkers, or you need to clear tree limbs or another obstacle

- Know the flight-to-roll ratio of the high wedge shot to choose an appropriate landing area on the green

- Know the clubface position you're trying to produce at impact

- Visualize and rehearse the shot

Swing Thoughts

- A high shot requires a high finish

- Stay back or "work under" to throw the ball higher in the air

- Swing with a smooth tempo on the backswing and forward swing

Practice Strategies

PITCHING

Accomplished golfers—and especially high handicappers—are presented several opportunities during a round to get the ball up and down with a wedge shot from inside 100 yards. Remember. . . one of the most important elements of practicing wedge shots is to know the yardage of your targets on the practice range. Your mind and body can store the swing of a particular distance during your practice sessions so you can call it up from memory when faced with a shot from the same distance on the golf course.

Fundamental Drill

Clearly, the ideal situation for practicing wedge shots is at a short-game practice facility to a regulation green, but you can certainly practice wedge shots on the range as long as you set out some targets (like headcovers, for example) to known distances. Use the setup and swing keys in this chapter to practice your wedge shots. Start by hitting some standard wedge shots to the middle of the green. Make sure each swing has an even rhythm and tempo and a backswing and forward swing appropriate for the shot. Make sure you're producing solid, consistent contact. Then, start working to control trajectory with your pitch shots. Choose a situation around the green which requires a high, soft pitch over a bunker, for example. Next, hit low, running pitches to the back of the green. Finish up by hitting a few more standard trajectory shots to the middle of the green. Notice not only the trajectory of the different wedge shots, but how far, in general, the ball rolls once it lands.

Competitive Drill

Sharpen your skills under a little pressure and create a personal best score with the five-ball drill. You will hit wedge shots to three different targets with three different trajectories. Try to vary the distance of your targets from one practice session to the next. For example, you may choose to hit 20, 30 and 40 yard pitches one day and 50, 60 and 70 yard pitches the next. Choose your first target on the practice pitching green. Your goal is to score at least three points from five balls. Take one point for an acceptable shot and two points if you happen to hole the shot. You define the acceptable zone around the hole which rewards you with a point. Hit three series of balls to each target executing high, low and standard trajectory wedge shots. Keep a tally of successful shots and points scored. This drill will help you master almost any shot within 100 yards of the green.

THE ONE-LEVER FLOP

No Room to Work With

"Golf is a game of endless predicaments."
—Chi-Chi Rodriguez

Every golfer who has ever worked with me knows how much I value the short game. You need good ball-striking for consistency, but let's face it, even the very best Tour professionals average only 13 out of 18 greens in regulation. So the difference between making and missing cuts or winning and finishing well back in the pack often comes down to the short game. And there's no more nerve-racking or spectacular short shot than the flop shot. You look to the flop shot when you don't have much green to work with. It flies high and lands soft and can be a master key to get you out of jail.

Almost everyone knows that Phil Mickelson is a master of the flop shot. Phil grew up with a regulation green in his backyard. He spent hours every day working on a variety of flop shots, and it shows. Another player whose flop shot doesn't always get the recognition it deserves is Tiger Woods. At the 1999 Western Open, Tiger was in the lead but being closely pursued when he made the turn on the final day. His approach at the tenth hole flew over the green. Now he was faced with a 50-foot shot over the corner of a bunker to a pin tucked at the front of the green. Most players would have played a safe pitch to the left of the hole, but Tiger played a magnificent flop shot that floated high over the bunker, landed just short of the pin and rolled to within tap-in distance. He never looked back after that, going on to win the tournament.

Many amateurs have an unreasonable fear of the flop shot. The simple reason they are scared of the flop shot, however, is because they don't know the techniques to master it. In all my years of working with players from beginners to Tour professionals, I've learned that there are three ways of hitting the flop shot. We'll start with the one that can get you going the fastest and then work from there.

As you learn these techniques, don't forget—as with all the shots in this book—to integrate them into your practice routine. It's very difficult to play a shot you've never practiced before. With flop shots, it's almost impossible.

The reason I teach three different ways to play the flop shot is because no two on-course situations are ever the same. Lie, distance and amount of green to work with can greatly influence shot selection around the green. Each of these three flop shots you're going to learn has its place. Only when you know them all will you be able to develop an instinct for which shot works best when. And a golfer with a good instinct for the short game is a golfer who can score.

FEATURED SHOT: THE ONE-LEVER FLOP

The one-lever flop shot is easy to play and incorporates all the basic adjustments required for any flop shot. In this swing, you will minimize the role of the wrists, meaning you don't have to time the release quite as perfectly as the other flop shots we'll look at later. It's a perfect shot for popping the ball up over a small bunker or over the collar to a pin cut close to the fringe. This shot works best from the fairway or a first cut of rough, when you don't have to fly the ball very far.

Start with a sand wedge or lob wedge. Loft is crucial to good flop shots, so I don't recommend a pitching wedge in this situation. Now open the clubface. The number one fault I see in high-handicappers who have trouble hitting the flop shot is that they fail to open the club-face enough. Instead, they attempt to play the shot with a square club-face and usually end up scooping at the ball with their hands and wrists in an effort to help it into the air. With a wedge in your hands, scooping almost always leads to disaster—skulled or fat shots. So start preparing for the flop shot by opening your clubface. How much you open the face depends on how much loft and distance you need.

Use the wedge's leading edge to align to the target. The target line should be perpendicular to the leading edge. After aligning the club-face to the target, grip down one or two inches on the handle and hold the club lightly in both hands. This is a finesse shot, and you'll need to feel as much of the weight of the clubhead as possible.

Now take your address. Stand closer to the ball—about the same distance closer as you gripped down on the handle—since this shot requires a steeper swing angle. Your body should be in an open posi-

tion. How much of an open body you need is determined by how open the clubface is. Distribute your weight evenly between the left and right sides, with your stance about the width of your hips. Play the ball one or two inches forward from the center of your stance. This helps set your body in the proper position to hit a high, soft shot. Position your hands about even with the ball. Ideally, the clubhead and handle of the club will arrive at the ball at the same time.

I call this shot the one-lever flop because it calls for a one-lever swing. By that I mean you don't break your wrists as you swing back. Instead, you use the arms to

For good flop shots, open the blade of your wedge, but be sure to align the leading edge of the clubhead to the target.

The one-lever flop features minimal wrist break and is great for soft shots from short distances.

swing the club back along the line of your shoulders. Control distance with the length of the swing. Then swing through the ball, sliding the clubface underneath. Accelerate the club on the forward swing to create a high, spinning shot. I tell my students to try to thump the ground with the clubhead. This helps you work the clubhead down into the ball.

The key to this shot is the "hit-and-resist" finish. Hold the one-lever position through the impact area to keep from releasing the club and closing the clubface and concentrate on finishing with the club in front of your body. A good visual here is to imagine that you are balancing a glass of water on the clubface in the finish position. Allow your lower body to respond to your upper body on the finish, always keeping your arms in front of your body.

With a little bit of practice, you can be hitting the one-lever flop this weekend. Work on distance control using the length and pace of the swing as your measures. This is a shot you'll come to love.

THE GOOD-HANDS FLOP SHOT

While I like the one-lever flop shot for its consistency and its simplicity around the green, there are times when it just won't work. Maybe you're in heavier rough or on a tight lie, or you need to get more spin on the ball to stop it on a finger of the green. To get the ball up quickly and make it stop when it lands, you're going to need to use your hands to create a steeper, more vertical swing. I call this the good-hands flop shot. This is the flop shot that most Tour professionals play.

For this shot, you'll use your hands and hinge your wrists much earlier to swing the club back into position, as you would for a regular greenside bunker shot.

The setup essentials are the same here as they were for the one-lever shot. First, open the clubface as much as you need to, grip down an inch or two to shorten the club and add control and grip the club lightly, again so that you can feel the weight of the clubhead in your hands. Stand a little closer to the ball and align your body in an open position corresponding to the open clubface.

The good-hands flop flies farther because of a longer swing with more hand and wrist action. Finish with the clubface still in the open position pointing to the sky.

The swing is slightly longer and faster than it was for the one-lever flop. Hinge your wrists early as you take the club away, minimizing the arm swing so that you feel the club working up immediately as it moves away from the ball. Swing the clubhead up and along the line of your shoulders.

By using your hands and wrists on the takeaway, you'll naturally swing the club into a higher position. At the top, the shaft should be just about vertical, with the butt end of the club pointing almost straight down at the ground.

It is crucial to a good hands-based flop shot that you hold the clubface in an open position all the way through the impact zone. In other words, this is also a hit-and-resist situation, so be sure to hold on to the club as you swing down and into the ground, preventing the face from closing as you swing through the hitting area. Control the distance of this shot by the length of the follow-through: A short follow-through for a short shot and a full follow-through for the longest flop shot.

THE CUT FLOP

Occasionally you will need to play a shot from thick grass near the green that requires enough clubhead speed to get the ball moving and spinning but does not fly more than just a few feet. This is a perfect situation for the cut flop.

A word of warning on this shot: it takes timing and precision to play properly. The cut flop will not work from all lies. In fact, I've seen some of the finest short-game players I know attempt this shot when the ball is sitting up in longer grass only to slide the clubface completely underneath the ball, not advancing it an inch. That said, however, I really like the cut flop because it produces a lot of spin. You can use it when pitching downhill or when you need to be aggressive even though you only have a few yards to cover.

As with all flop shots, start with an open clubface. Grip down an inch or even two for shorter shots and use a very light grip pressure. This is the ultimate touch shot. Stand an inch or two closer to the ball and line your body well to the left of the target. Now swing back on an exaggerated outside path, with the arms working away from the body and up, to about a three-quarters position. Swing back down the same path.

The exaggerated out-to-in swing of this shot means that you'll contact the ball toward the toe of the clubface, hitting it with a glancing blow. Pull your arms in toward your body as you swing through the impact area to impact left-to-right cut spin on the ball. Allow your left elbow to bend into a "chicken-wing" position after impact. The ball will shoot up steeply and will land softly on the green.

FLOP SHOP

The very best short-game players have all three of the flop shots we've discussed in this chapter. Each has its specific uses and purposes. But I also know many very good players who use only one of

The exaggerated outside-in path of the cut flop creates a lot of spin for the tightest situations.

these flop shots almost exclusively. The bottom line is that you have to practice each of the shots to know which is most comfortable for you in what situations.

If you have no confidence with flop shots, start with the one-lever flop and work your way to the other two. But make sure the flop shot is a part of your greenside repertoire. You'll be glad you did.

Chapter Summary

THE ONE-LEVER FLOP

Setup

- Open the clubface of the sand or lob wedge and align it to the target

- Open the entire body a corresponding amount

- Grip down one to two inches

- Stand one to two inches closer to the ball

- Lighter than normal grip pressure in both hands for good touch or "feel"

- Distribute weight evenly between left and right

- Stance is the width of your hips

- Ball position dictated by the lie: one inch more forward than normal for a good lie, normal or just left of center for an average lie, one inch back of center if the ball is down in the grass slightly

Swing

- Minimize the role of the wrists in the backswing and forward swing

- Use the arms to swing the club back along the line of your shoulders

- Swing down and through the ball at a descending angle, sliding the clubface underneath the ball

- The clubhead and handle arrive at the ball at the same time

- Hold the one-lever position through the impact area to keep from releasing the club and closing the clubface—finish with the club in front of you, clubface to the sky

- Allow lower body to respond to upper body on the finish, keeping arms in front of the body

- Tempo and rhythm equal for backswing and forward swing

Strategy

- This shot is great if you have a short distance to carry the ball, but need it to land softly and stop quickly once it hits the ground, like a delicate pitch over the collar of a green that is sloped severely away from you

- Distance is controlled by the length and pace of the swing and the clubface position

- Know how far the ball carries and rolls with different swing lengths and with the differing amounts you open clubface and body

Swing Thoughts

- Relaxed hands and arms

- Thump the ground on the forward swing

- Hit-and-resist finish

THE GOOD-HANDS FLOP

Setup

- Open the clubface of the sand or lob wedge and align it to the target

- Open the entire body a corresponding amount

- Grip down one to two inches

- Stand one to two inches closer to the ball

- Lighter than normal grip pressure in both hands for good touch or "feel"

- Distribute weight evenly between left and right

- Stance is the width of your hips

- Ball position dictated by the lie: one inch more forward than normal for a good lie, normal or just left of center for an average lie, one inch back of center if the ball is down in the grass slightly

Swing

- Swing is slightly longer and faster than the one-lever flop

- Hinge the wrists early as you take the club away, minimizing the amount of arm swing so you feel the clubhead working up as you take the club back

- Swing the club up and along the line of your shoulders

- At the top, the club is almost vertical with the butt of the handle pointing to the ground

- Swing down and through the ball at a descending angle, sliding the clubface underneath the ball

- The clubhead and handle arrive at the ball at the same time

- Hit and resist is also key: hold the clubface in an open position through the impact area and on to the finish to keep from closing the clubface

- Allow lower body to respond to upper body on the finish, keeping arms in front of the body

Strategy

- This shot is great if you have to carry the ball farther than a few feet, but need it to land softly and stop quickly once it hits the ground, such as a delicate pitch over a bunker to a tight pin placement, or if you're in heavier rough or on a very tight lie

- Control distance with the amount of follow-through—a short follow-through for a short shot and a full follow-through for a longer flop shot

- Know how far the ball carries and rolls with different swing lengths and with the differing amounts you open clubface and body

Swing Thoughts

- Relaxed hands and arms

- Maintain an open clubface on the forward swing—clubface to the sky

- Club works down into the ground

- Controlled finish

THE CUT FLOP

Setup

- Open the clubface of the sand or lob wedge and align it to the target

- Open the entire body a corresponding amount

- Grip down one to two inches

- Stand one to two inches closer to the ball

- Lighter than normal grip pressure in both hands for good touch or "feel"

- Distribute weight evenly between left and right

- Stance is the width of your hips

- Ball position dictated by the lie: one inch more forward than normal for a good lie, normal or just left of center for an average lie, one inch back of center if the ball is down in the grass slightly

Swing

- Swing the club back on an exaggerated outside path, arms working away from the body as they swing up

- Hinge the club up to a three-quarters position in the backswing

- Swing down and through the ball along the same out-to-in path

- Slide the clubface across the ball, contacting the ball on the toe of the club

- Pull your arms in toward your body on the forward swing to impart left-to-right cut spin on the ball

- Allow your left elbow to bend into a "chicken-wing" position after impact, holding the clubface in an open position through the hitting area to keep from closing the clubface

- Allow your lower body to pivot in response to the arm swing on the forward swing

Strategy

- This shot is perfect if you have to swing aggressively enough to get the ball out of superthick rough, but need a lot of spin so the ball stops quickly once it hits the ground

- Be cautious with this one: it's easy to slide the clubface under the ball, barely moving it

- Know how far the ball carries and rolls with different swing lengths and with the differing amounts you open clubface and body

Swing Thoughts

- "Cut" the ball out of the grass, arms pull in on the forward swing

- Maintain an open clubface on the forward swing—clubface to the sky

Practice Strategies
THE FLOP SHOT

This shot takes a fair amount of practice and a lot of imagination to pull off successfully on the golf course. Time spent around the green practicing the one-lever flop and the good-hands flop, however, will familiarize you with the situations that suit each shot so you can execute a high, soft shot when you need one.

Fundamental Drill

Use the setup and swing adjustments in this chapter to produce the one-lever flop, the good-hands flop and the cut flop. Choose situations around the green that call for each particular shot. The one-lever flop is used when the ball is fairly close to the green with a relatively small obstacle to carry or just the collar of rough to a close-cut pin. Choose a shot that requires a little more carry and start experimenting with the good-hands flop, which allows you to lever the club up on the backswing and the forward swing, creating a little longer swing. Finally, find some long grass and use the cut flop technique. Your task is to produce solid contact and effectively control distance and trajectory with each shot. You'll be creating realistic situations around the green from different lies and learning your capabilities with each shot. You'll also be exercising your imagination and creativity—both of which are vital to executing these shots. Choose a very specific landing area and make note of how far the ball releases once it lands. Experiment opening the clubface and your body, and with the length and pace of the swing to produce shots with varying trajectories. You'll probably develop a favorite way to approach flop shots that will most predictably allow you to control carry and roll.

Competitive Drill

Once again the five-ball drill is your friend when practicing the flop shot. Choose three situations around the green—one for each of the three different flop shots. You should pick a situation that calls for the specific shot you're practicing. Give yourself three attempts to score three of five points. Create a scoring zone appropriate for your skill level to award points. Of course, if you hole one, give yourself two points!

ELEVEN

THE SPLASH SHOT

Playing in the Sand

"There is an old saying: If a man comes home with sand in his cuffs and cockleburs in his pants, don't ask him what he shot."

—Sam Snead

Golf is full of difficult shots and situations. Fortunately, a sand bunker shot doesn't have to be one of them. Whether you must deal with a greenside bunker, a long bunker approach or a fairway bunker, good technique and confidence will help you get out surely and safely. Tour professionals routinely get the ball up and down—the leading players save par about 70 percent of the time from greenside bunkers. A number of my professional students will actually aim for a greenside bunker on longer par-5 holes, figuring that the bunker shot provides a better opportunity to get the ball close to the hole than a shot from deep grass does. Still, the average player wastes shots every round by not understanding how to play from the sand.

In this chapter, I'll show you a foolproof way of escaping the sand. Then you'll learn to tailor your sand game to the conditions you encounter on the course. By practicing the techniques and drills in this chapter, you'll come to realize that bunkers aren't the monsters that course designers would have you believe they are. Just treat them with respect and authority, and they should give you no trouble at all.

FEATURED SHOT: THE BASIC SPLASH

The problem that keeps many golfers from developing consistency and confidence in the bunkers is a misunderstanding of the most fundamental element of the sand shot—that you slide the clubface underneath the ball. In other words, you never even hit the ball! Far too many weekend golfers try to "pick" the ball out of the sand and end up scooping with their hands, hitting far behind the ball and failing to get it out or, worse, blading the ball and sending it rocketing over the green and into deeper trouble. Or they try to overpower the ball with a violent blast that offers no consistency or control. If these sound like problems you face in your own game, take heart. If you develop the basic splash shot from the sand, you'll never be in too much trouble when your ball winds up in a bunker. You'll frustrate your opponents by routinely escaping trouble, and you'll have the confidence you need to fire at pins without letting fear of the sand change your game plan.

The splash shot assumes that you're in a typical bunker situation—the ball is sitting up on dry sand, and you have enough room to make an unrestricted swing. Special conditions such as wet sand, longer shots, uneven lies and buried lies require adjustments I'll discuss later, but good sand play starts with being able to handle the most common scenario.

The Setup

A proper setup is essential, since the goal is to hit the sand and not the ball. The setup lays the foundation for everything that follows. Here's a simple checklist to make sure you've set up well for the basic greenside bunker shot.

For the basic "splash" shot, play the ball forward and open the face of the sand wedge.

Open the face of the sand wedge for maximum bounce and loft. It may look a little strange at first, but an open clubface is something that all good sand players have in common. Use your normal grip, holding the club at the end of the handle. Gripping down will raise the bottom point of the swing, putting you at risk for thin shots. Remember, the goal will be to slide the clubhead underneath the ball. Grip pressure for this shot is very light in order to promote an easy hinging of the wrists during the backswing.

Open your body until the leading edge of the clubface is aligned perpendicular with the target. Shorter shots where the face is most open will likewise require the most open alignment. Widen your stance slightly and play the ball a little forward with more weight on your left side.

Dig into the sand with both feet for stability. Digging into the sand isn't just to make you look like a pro—it also redefines the bottom of your swing arc to a point just beneath the ball. If you dig two inches

The leading edge of the wedge aims at the target, with your body in an open position.

deep in the sand, for example, you should automatically hit two inches behind and under the ball.

These setup adjustments normalize the swing that follows. You've now given your body a signal that you're ready to splash.

The Splash Swing

Since you never hit the ball during a splash shot, your swing from a greenside bunker needs to be longer than it would be for a shot of equal distance from grass. You also have to be absolutely sure that you accelerate through the ball and swing down and through the sand.

The backswing is controlled by the upper body, using the arms and shoulders while the lower body remains "quiet." Hinge your wrists early in the backswing. By setting your wrists, you are creating a V-shaped arc instead of the flatter U-shape of a full swing. This sets up a steeper, more descending angle into the sand.

The backswing for the "splash" shot is more vertical with the hands and arms.

Make sure your swing is fluid and relaxed. Rhythm is the most important element. Concentrate on making a smooth transition from the backswing into the forward swing, letting your hands lead the clubhead.

Concentrate on holding the clubface open through impact. The head of the sand wedge will splash the surface of the bunker and slide just under the ball so that the ball rides out on a thin wave of sand. The momentum of the swing will carry you into a nice, balanced follow-through with your weight on the left side, belt buckle pointing left of the target and right heel off the ground.

If there is one mental tip that I think helps people play better from bunkers, it is to picture throwing sand onto the green with each swing. This makes sure that you have made a full follow-through. Do this and you will almost always get the ball out of the bunker and onto the green in one shot.

You need to swing through to a longer finish because the sand adds more resistance than grass.

Distance Control

The distance you get from the bunker depends on your address and the length of the swing. For short bunker shots, open your clubface and body a little more to hit the ball higher. Dig a bit deeper at address so that you will take more sand. Make a pronounced V-shaped swing, swinging the club a little shorter both back and through.

When faced with a longer shot, align both the clubface and your body in less open positions, more toward the target. Play the ball slightly back, toward the center of your stance. Dig your feet just enough to provide stability. Now make a longer, U-shaped backswing with a more complete follow-through.Stay aggressive and be sure to complete your follow-through. Quitting on a sand shot means staying in the bunker.

Sand Conditions and Other Factors

Sand conditions also call for adjustments. If the sand is extremely light and fluffy, you'll have to guard against digging too far under the ball. Grip down an inch or two on the grip and distribute your weight evenly at address. Play the ball just off your left heel and dig just enough to stabilize your feet. This will prevent you from swinging down too steeply. Make a wider, more U-shaped swing, allowing your wrists to hinge naturally. These adjustments will help you keep your momentum through impact and will minimize the effects of the fluffy sand.

Conversely, if the sand is hard or wet, you'll want to avoid having the clubhead bounce off the sand and into the ball. Consider using a pitching wedge. Since a pitching wedge has less bounce, it will dig under the ball, reducing the chance of a bladed shot. If you choose a sand wedge, square up the clubface to de-emphasize the bounce of the club and make a steeper "V"-shaped swing. Play the ball in the middle of your stance and set more weight on your left side at address. Allow for a lower trajectory on the shot and more roll.

You should also factor weather and course conditions into your preshot planning. If the wind is in your face, you should fly the ball almost all the way to the hole. When the wind is at your back—even

The length of the follow-through determines the distance of the shot. A short shot requires a shorter follow-through while a longer shot requires a more complete finish.

on a short bunker shot—the ball will tend to roll more when it lands. What is the green like? Is it hard or soft? Does it slope into you or away from you? These factors are crucial as you decide how far you must hit the shot in the air in order to get it close to the flagstick.

If the conditions conspire against you, don't be afraid to play away from the flagstick. The last thing you want to do is get cute and leave the ball in the bunker. Now you've wasted a shot, and you're still stuck in the same predicament. As any professional player can tell you, the difference between bogey and double bogey or worse is much more than just one or two strokes. Job one is to get the ball back into position to avoid the big number.

THE SAND WEDGE

You wouldn't try to build a bridge without the right tools, and you'll need the right tool to build a good sand game as well. So take a few minutes and get to know your sand wedge. Gene Sarazen, one of the greatest bunker players of all time, invented the sand wedge after discovering that he could control the ball much better by taking a shallow divot when playing from the sand. If he could keep the club from digging into the sand, he could get a better trajectory and much more spin on the ball. So he took a regular pitching wedge and added a flange into the design. The flange provided a characteristic called bounce, and the sand wedge soon became standard equipment in every player's bag.

I recommend that all players carry a sand wedge with 54 or 56 degrees of loft and 6 to 12 degrees of bounce. What exactly is bounce, and how does it play into your bunker shots? Look at the bottom of your sand wedge. The angle formed by the rear of the flange and the back of the clubface represents the bounce. When you strike the sand, bounce prevents digging. The leading edge of the club slips underneath the ball. The bounce then causes the clubface to rise back toward the surface of the sand, splashing the ball out and onto the green and allowing you to get spin and control even though you haven't hit the ball in the traditional sense.

The more bounce, the less likely you are to dig under the ball when attempting a greenside bunker shot. If the bunkers on your home course are filled with light, fluffy sand, you should choose a sand wedge with more bounce. If the sand is thin and there is a hard surface underneath, choose a sand wedge with less bounce. Remember that you can alter the characteristics of your sand wedge by face position. The more open the face, the more bounce you'll have.

Once you find a sand wedge you like, stick with it. Most of the Tour players I work with have had their sand wedges so long that the grooves have begun to wear away on the face. Take a look at a good player's sand wedge. If you see the telltale signs of thousands of bunker shots, you can bet you're looking at a good sand player.

ADVANCED GREENSIDE BUNKER PLAY

The splash shot will get you safely out of most bunker situations, but certain conditions require special considerations and adjustments. Using the standard techniques for the splash shot as a starting point, here are some guidelines for becoming an outstanding sand player.

Recognize a Trap

The United States Golf Association never uses the term "sand trap." But as all golfers know, that's exactly what some bunkers are. You should be able to spot the most severe bunkers from 180 yards. Then do everything you can to avoid them.

Here are some familiar bunker traps.

Sand Facing Water   The most famous example is the short but murderous 12th hole at Augusta National Golf Club. With water and sand short of the extremely shallow green, players want to be sure to take enough club. But if they play it too safely, they'll find the rear bunker. Now they're faced with a downhill bunker shot back toward the water. Not a pretty sight.

The Pot Bunker Pete Dye borrowed the pot bunker concept from the old links courses of Scotland, and now you'll find these troublesome little pits on courses throughout America. The problem with pot bunkers is that they generally have very steep faces and a small surface area of sand. You almost always have to alter your stance or swing. Architects often use pot bunkers opposite a big, gaping bunker that you will instinctively play away from, even though it is by far the lesser of the two evils.

The High Lip: It's common to find a bunker with a very high lip fronting the green of a short par-4 or par-5. Since you're hitting your approach with a short iron or wedge, the architect wants to challenge your depth perception, forcing you to clear a significant obstacle. If you fail, your high approach shot will likely bury in the face of the bunker. The third hole at Cherry Hills Country Club in Denver is a perfect example. It's only about 310 yards long, and the green is surrounded by bunkers. But it's the bunker in front that is the big no-no. The high lip is the architect's way of giving teeth to an otherwise easy hole.

You won't always be able to play around the toughest bunkers, but as Sam Snead once said, "Knowing where to miss the ball is half of good golf."

BUNKER RULES AND ETIQUETTE

The Rules of Golf consider bunkers to be hazards. That means you cannot ground your club at address or hit the sand on your back-swing. You can only touch the sand as part of the downswing. Likewise, you can't take a practice swing to test the texture of the sand. A couple of years ago, Senior Tour player Jerry McGee found himself in a bunker on the 71st hole of a tournament. After muffing his shot and leaving it in the bunker, he took a quick and disgusted practice swing before stepping up to play his next shot. The one-shot penalty turned his already costly double bogey into a triple.

Be sure to familiarize yourself with the local rules of the courses you play. Many courses today feature sandy waste areas. These waste areas are not considered hazards, though at first glance they may appear to be bunkers. You play waste areas just as you would any other part of the golf course, meaning you can take practice swings and ground your club if you wish. I usually have my students treat these areas just like bunkers, however, to maintain consistency of technique. Always assume that a sandy area is a hazard unless you know for sure that it's not.

Finally, you'll do yourself, your fellow competitors and the rest of the players on the course a big favor by learning the etiquette of bunkers. Always enter the bunker from the low side. You won't damage the lip or displace the sand as you would if you were to come down the face of a bunker. Carry a rake into the bunker with you. After your shot, rake your divot and footprints thoroughly with a back-and-forth motion, leaving the sand as flat as possible. Exit by following the footprints you made on your way in, raking as you go. Most courses request that you leave the rake in or at the edge of the bunker, away from any other rakes.

THE BUNKER PITCH:
THE MOST DIFFICULT SHOT IN GOLF

Now that you've got a good idea of how to play any greenside bunker shot, you can begin to work on a shot that even the best players in the world have trouble mastering—the 50–100 yard bunker shot. You'll often encounter these short bunkers on par-5 holes and shorter par-4 holes, where architects place them to punish gamblers who bite off more than they can chew.

When faced with a bunker shot of 50–100 yards, most golfers simply square up the face of their sand wedges and swing away, often with disastrous results. It doesn't have to be that way.

Preparing for the Shot

Your main goal when faced with the long bunker approach is simply to get the ball on the green. Getting the ball close to the hole with a 50–100 yard bunker shot is a bonus, even for touring professionals.

Start with club selection. I like to use anywhere from a pitching wedge to an 8-iron, depending on how far you need to hit the ball. After making your club selection, open up the clubface and play the shot much like a regular greenside bunker shot, "splashing" the sand to produce a longer shot.

The setup and alignment techniques are virtually identical to a greenside bunker shot, except you need to grip down about an inch on the club. Use your familiarity with the technique to help you relax and feel comfortable and confident. You're not trying anything here that you don't already know how to do.

The Swing

The swing itself resembles the up-and-down, V-shape of the green-side bunker shot. Since you're using a club with less loft, you will produce a lower trajectory and more distance than a normal bunker shot. Swing the club back and through with the upper body—the hands, arms, and shoulders. Keep your lower body passive, allowing it to follow the arms and upper body. Control the distance you get on the shot by the length and pace of your swing—for a full shot, swing the club about three-quarters of the way back for better control. Again, think of splashing the sand and sliding the clubface underneath the ball. Swing through into a well-balanced finish, with the weight on the left side and right heel off the ground. Your hips should remain level, with the belt buckle facing slightly left of the target. As you evaluate the results, remember again that anything on the green or fringe is a pretty good shot. The goal is simply to recover and move on.

Unfortunately, there is no other way to master this shot than to repeat it over and over. Try different clubs—perhaps a 9-iron or pitching wedge—to better judge distances. But if you're patient and work at it, you'll find yourself scoring better on those reachable par-5s and par-4s, because you'll know you can recover from the bunker guarding the green.

THE FAIRWAY BUNKER SHOT

Fairway bunkers present a completely different challenge than greenside bunkers. When playing from a fairway bunker, you've got to be sure to contact the ball first. Again, resist the urge to pick the ball off of the sand. That's a low percentage shot. You'll end up hitting the ball thin, bringing the lip of the bunker into play and risking leaving yourself in really deep trouble. Or you'll try to help the ball into the air, hit behind it, and get a shot that barely clears the bunker, failing to improve your position and leaving you yet another difficult approach.

Fortunately, good fairway bunker play is well within your reach. Here's how.

Evaluate the Shot

The first step in a successful fairway bunker shot is a thorough analysis of the situation. Two items are especially important: the lie of the ball and the height of the bunker's lip. These factors dictate the type of shot you will be able to play.

Be realistic when assessing your lie. If the ball is sitting too far down in the sand or is in a position that does not allow you to take an adequate stance or swing, you may opt to splash or blast out to the fairway. The goal is to get the ball back into play with a single stroke.

If the lie is suitable, and you elect to hit a full shot, check the lip of the bunker. The higher the lip, the more loft you will need on your shot. Ask yourself what is appropriate. If you have a long iron to the green, and the bunker has a steep lip, you should fall back to a more lofted club and play to a target short of the green. As you consider the lip, keep in mind that the stance and swing adjustments you make will produce a shot that flies slightly lower than normal. If you have any doubts whether you have enough loft to clear the lip or not, go with the more lofted club.

However, if the lip is not a major issue, you will probably need to adjust club selection in the other direction. Since the proper technique for the fairway bunker shot involves less lower-body movement and a slightly shortened swing, you should add a club to what you would normally hit. If you hit a 7-iron 150 yards off the grass you will likely need a 6-iron to cover the same distance from a bunker. The harder you swing in a bunker, the greater the chance of mistakes. Choose a club that allows you to make a smooth, controlled swing.

If you have a long fairway bunker shot, you should consider using a wood. A lofted wood such as a 7- or a 5-wood, particularly the new shallow-faced models that are available today, is much easier to hit from a bunker than a long iron. You'll get better trajectory and distance, and the soleplate of the wood provides great protection against digging. Just be sure to grip down a couple of inches and resist the urge to overpower it.

After analyzing your situation and selecting the proper club, you're ready to play the shot. Good luck!

Setup and Swing

Grip down about an inch on the club. This will help you control the club during the swing so that you will not dig into the sand before striking the ball. Remember that gripping down will also serve to decrease distance—another reason to add a club to fairway bunker shots.

Widen your stance. The best swing for ensuring that you hit the ball cleanly is one in which the lower body remains stable and "quiet." By widening your stance you restrict the movement of the hips and legs, reducing the chances of the disastrous fat shot. Play the

In a fairway bunker, widen your stance, set up with the ball in the middle of your stance, then grip down about an inch, and dig in with your left foot. These adjustments help you hit the ball first.

ball in the middle of your stance. This sets you up to strike the ball first.

Dig into the sand with your left foot only, setting more weight on the left side. Again, this serves to keep the lower body from moving throughout the swing. Tap down with your right foot to create a solid base, but don't dig the right foot into the sand. Should you be faced with an uneven lie , be sure your spine is set perpendicular to the slope of the ground.

Make a three-quarters arm swing back and through. Clean contact—not power—is the objective. You have set up to minimize lower-body activity. Therefore, you should shorten your swing so that you don't force the lower body into motion. A three-quarters swing provides plenty of power. Focus on tempo. The swing should be smooth, relaxed and controlled and should lead into a well-balanced finish. Imagine that you are hitting the ball off a cart path, trying to just graze the ground. By doing this, you'll get a feel for the trajectory and distance of the fairway bunker shot.

A FINAL WORD ON BUNKERS

This chapter will go a long way toward helping you develop a solid sand game—at your home course. The rub is that the sand at each course is very different. In Florida, for example, you may encounter fine-grain river sand in the northern part of the state and coarse beach sand in other parts. The type of sand will likely have some effect on the behavior of the ball, particularly on greenside bunker shots.

A three-quarters backswing will help keep the lower body quiet for better balance in the loose sand.

I always urge my students—from beginners to Tour pros—to spend some time in the practice bunker at any course they are required to play. With good technique, your brain and body will make the small adjustments within just a few shots. Make sure you give yourself a chance to adapt before you are on the course. It only takes a few minutes to acclimate to local sand, and it's an investment that is well worthwhile.

Chapter Summary

THE GREENSIDE BUNKER SPLASH SHOT

Setup

- Open the face of the sand wedge one-quarter turn to maximize the loft and bounce of the club

- Using your full-swing grip, hold the club at the end of the grip

- Light grip pressure in both hands

- Open your body until the clubface aligns with the target

- Play the ball forward with your weight anchored on your left side

- Dig into the sand for stability and to lower the bottom of the swing

Swing

- You must hit the sand before the ball to slide the clubface under the ball

- Because you hit the sand before the ball, the swing needs to be longer than for a shot of equal distance from grass

- Swing itself is mostly upper body

- Swing the club back along the line of your body (outside the target line)

- Hinge your wrists early to create a steeper, more descending blow

- Make a smooth transition from backswing to forward swing

- Hold the clubface open through the hitting area

- Make a balanced finish: weight on the left side, belt buckle to the target and right heel off the ground

- Control distance by the amount you open the clubface and body and the length and pace of your swing

Strategy

- You're trying to allow the head of the sand wedge to splash the surface of the bunker and slide under the ball so that the ball rides out on a thin wave of sand

- Choose a sand wedge with an appropriate-size flange and the right amount of bounce: big bounce and flange for fine, fluffy sand; smaller flange and less bounce for coarse, heavy sand or sparsely filled bunkers

- Evaluate the lie, sand conditions, height of the lip and pin placement

- Rehearse the shot as you imagine it outside the bunker

- Some players focus on the ball, others on the sand a few inches behind the ball—experiment to see which allows you to splash the ball out more consistently

Swing Thoughts

- Stay relaxed—smooth tempo on the backswing and forward swing

- Imagine hitting the sand, throwing sand onto the green with your swing

THE FAIRWAY BUNKER SHOT

Setup

- Consider the lip of the bunker and the distance to your target for club selection. You'll need to use a club with enough loft to clear the lip, but if the lip isn't a factor, use one extra club because the setup and swing changes for this shot reduce overall distance

- Grip down one inch

- Widen stance slightly to restrict lower-body motion

- Play the ball in the middle of your stance to make sure you strike the ball first

- Dig into the sand with the left foot only to set weight left for a quiet lower body and slightly descending blow

Swing

- You're trying to hit the ball, then graze the sand

- Take a three-quarters backswing

- Swing generated primarily by the upper body

- Concentrate on keeping the lower body quiet

- Make a smooth, controlled swing focusing on solid contact

- Make a full, well-balanced finish

Strategy

- Assess the lie and height of the lip; do you have room for an adequate stance and swing or would you be better off splashing the ball out and back in play with a wedge?

- The higher the lip, the more loft you'll need

- The setup and swing adjustments for a fairway bunker shot make for a lower trajectory—take that into consideration when selecting a club to clear the lip

- Avoid the "thin" shot that may not have the height required to clear the lip

- Rehearse the shot as you imagine it outside the bunker

- Avoid the urge to overpower the ball

Swing Thoughts

- Stay relaxed—smooth tempo on the backswing and forward swing

- Clean contact—not power—is the objective

Practice Strategies

BUNKER PLAY

The greenside bunker shot is really one of the easiest shots in golf because: 1) you have a club with design characteristics especially for this shot, and 2) you have a wide margin for error because you don't even have to hit the ball! Use the following drills to help you experience how the design of the sand wedge helps pop the ball out of the sand and how to gauge the proper amount of sand to splash the ball out of the bunker. You don't have to fear the sand. All it takes is a little practice.

Fundamental Drill

Use the concepts and the setup and swing adjustments in this chapter to hit greenside and fairway bunker shots. To practice greenside bunker shots, draw a pie-plate-size circle around a ball in the sand. Your goal as you hit the shot is to enter the sand at the back edge of the circle, throwing the ball and a "plate" of sand out of the bunker at the same time. Learn to take the right amount of sand, skipping the sand wedge under the ball, creating a shallow divot, not dig. Be sure you finish with the clubhead in a nice high position and a complete finish to the target. Use the setup and swing adjustments in this chapter to control the distance of your greenside bunker shots. Pay attention to the starting direction of your shots and how much the ball rolls when it hits the ground.

When you can, practice fairway bunker shots by referencing the setup and swing changes highlighted in this chapter. Sometimes your only option for practice is to take advantage of a fairway bunker on the golf course from time to time and drop a couple of balls down to practice. Make sure you experience not only irons but also fairway woods out of fairway bunkers.

Competitive Drill

Use the five-ball drill to keep track of your progress in bunker play. For greenside bunkers (and fairway bunkers, if possible), hit three out of five acceptable shots from each situation. Use three attempts to reach your goal and record your personal best.

THE

RESTRICTED

SWING

Playing Your Way Out of Trouble

*"In golf I'm one under; one under a tree, one under a rock,
and one under a bush...."*

—Gerry Cheevers

No matter how good you are, golf will throw some unexpected situations your way and expect you to invent a way out of them. Spaniard Sergio Garcia came to the 1999 PGA Championship as a 19-year-old phenom. On the back nine of the final round he began a charge. Within the space of three holes he had picked up four shots on leader Tiger Woods, and when he came to the 16th hole, a ferocious 460-yard par-4, he stood just a single stroke off the lead. Garcia is a tremendously long hitter off the tee, but this time his length cost him as he drove through the fairway. The rough at Medinah Country Club was bad enough, but Garcia's ball bounded through the thick grass and settled right next to one of the 4,000 trees that line the course. The television announcers gave him no chance, telling the viewing audience that the teenage sensation would simply have to pitch out to the fairway. But Garcia had victory on his mind. Rather than playing it safe, he chose a 6-iron and swung away, closing his eyes as he drove down between the roots and into the ball. Miraculously, he made clean contact and sprinted down the fairway, leaping into the air in time to see his ball come to rest at the back of the putting surface. The entire golf world was stunned at the feat, and though Garcia eventually finished as runner-up to Woods, he had created a legend with his daring escape shot.

Most golfers will never find themselves faced with such a shot on a major championship Sunday, but you can bet that there will be times when your ball finds trouble and no standard swing or shot will get you out of it.

I've seen all sorts of escape shots, some successful and some not. And in some cases, I must say that I'd prefer to see the player take an unplayable lie rather than risk disaster or injury by attempting a miracle shot. But not all situations require miracle shots. Most simply require a little creative thinking and good execution. In this chapter, I'll show you how to escape some of golf's most common jail situations. You'll come out looking like a hero, but more importantly, a single bad break won't ruin a good round.

FEATURED SHOT: STOP-AND-GO—OUT OF THE TREES

In most parts of the world, the most prevalent of all on-course obstacles are trees. Though Sergio Garcia found the trunk and roots of the trees in his off-fairway adventure in Medinah, you're much more likely to encounter trees in the form of branches restricting your swing. Out-of-bounds fences and stakes can also restrict your swing, forcing you to strike the ball solidly using a swing that is quite different from your normal motion. In these cases, you need to know the stop-and-go escape shot.

If you're like most players, you've always tried to handle restricted shots by taking multiple practice swings, gradually reworking your swing until you don't hit the leaf or branch or stake. The problem is that when you try to hit the ball, you almost always revert to your standard swing and catch the object anyway, disrupting your timing and your confidence and altering the path of your swing, making it difficult to hit the ball. I've seen very good players totally whiff the ball when something interfered with their backswing.

The stop-and-go shot eliminates this problem by taking any potential surprises out of the swing.

Club Selection

While the stop-and-go shot is primarily designed to help you escape trouble and get the ball back in play, it can in fact be used to approach the green. The shot will behave much like a knockdown. First, assess the lie of the ball. Your first priority is to get the ball out from underneath the tree branches and into the fairway. The deeper the grass, the more loft you will need to get the ball into the air and out of trouble. Assuming that the lie is good, you will want to choose one or possibly even two more clubs than you would normally use from the same distance.

The stop-and-go shot helps you deal with overhanging tree limbs by keeping the clubhead from becoming tangled.

Setup

Grip down on the club one or two inches, or far enough to avoid the tree limbs above you. Move the ball about an inch back in your stance. Starting from a stop, you won't have as much speed on the swing, and you need to be sure to hit the ball first. Set up with your hands even or slightly ahead of the ball.

Swing to the top and stop. Now, take several forward swings, feeling the club, arms and body working together.

Executing the Shot

The problem with having your swing obstructed by limbs or an out-of-bounds fence or some other object comes in the transition between the backswing and the forward swing. For the stop-and-go shot, you'll eliminate the transition completely. Swing back to your stopping point, taking care to place the club in proper position. When you complete the backswing, hold your position until you are ready to start the forward swing. Now initiate the forward swing with the hands, arms and upper body all rotating down and through the ball.

The timing for this shot will require some practice on the range. But don't be afraid to try it. The stop-and-go is the most effective escape I know of from a restricted-swing situation.

To carry a steep lip, open the face of the club and play the ball forward in your stance, with your weight on the right side.

Against the Lip

In most fairway bunker situations, you can play a standard shot (see chapter 11 for more information). But occasionally you will find yourself in the front of the bunker, staring at a lip that is simply too high for you to be able to play a normal shot.

Let's say you are in a fairway bunker 150 yards from the green. You would normally hit a 7-iron from that distance, but that won't provide enough loft to get the ball over the lip of the bunker. How can you produce the trajectory you need to escape trouble along with the distance necessary to reach the target?

Start by selecting one to three clubs more than you would normally use from the same distance. Now open the clubface a quarter of a turn (about 45 degrees) and grip the club, gripping down about two inches to create a shorter lever and enhance control during the swing.

Widen your stance slightly to increase stability. A wider stance also limits lower-body movement during the swing, helping you maintain balance throughout the swing. Tilt your right shoulder to set your upper body slightly behind the ball.

The open clubface position, combined with your upper-body tilt, will produce a shot that climbs steeply into the air and moves from left to right. Be sure you have allowed for the fade by aligning yourself far enough left of the target.

Play the ball slightly forward in your stance. This ball position will help make sure that you hit the golf ball just as the clubhead begins to work its way up from the bottom point of the swing. Dig into the sand with your back foot only. This will set more weight on your right side, encouraging you to hit the ball just on the upswing. Tap your front foot slightly into the sand to create a solid base.

Make a three-quarters backswing to enhance control and balance. Swing on the tilt of your right shoulder, staying behind the ball. Concentrate on maintaining a smooth tempo on the forward swing. Try to feel yourself hanging back on your right side as you swing into the ball.

This shot, with its high trajectory and left-to-right shape, will give you plenty of distance and will stop quickly when it hits the green. Remember, the less lofted the club, the more the ball will fade.

You can also use this shot when your ball comes to rest in the bank of a steep hill with a grassy face. Anytime you need to get a long shot airborne quickly, this technique can help you escape and turn a trouble shot into a scoring opportunity.

The Explosion Shot

Just as you can encounter a restricted backswing when you find yourself in the trees, you can also face restricted follow-through shots. The most common of these is the buried lie in a bunker. The explosion shot is your way out. Not only is the explosion shot a must-have from the sand; you can also use it to play a ball partially submerged in water or one that is in high grass in the bank of a greenside bunker. The fundamentals of the explosion shot are the same, regardless of the situation.

Prepare yourself to play an explosion shot by first resetting your goals. The idea is to get the ball out of trouble and onto the much more predictable surface of the putting green or the fairway. If you are able to eliminate the big number, then you're becoming a good scrambler.

The explosion shot requires a sharply descending blow. Set up for this by gripping down two inches, standing two inches closer to the ball and playing the ball just to the right of the center of your stance, with your hands ahead of the ball. The key to ensuring a steep, descending blow is to set about 60 percent of your weight on your left side and leave it there throughout the swing.

Make a three-quarters backswing using only the hands, arms and shoulders to lift the club up sharply during the takeaway. Remember,

You can hit the explosion shot from grass, sand or water. Your weight starts left, stays left and finishes left, with the hands well ahead of the ball.

your weight starts left, stays left and finishes left. Swing down, leading with your hands and the handle of the club. Don't try to help the ball out. It's much more important to have a smooth forward swing tempo—the setup and swing changes will do all the necessary work. Strike the ground two to three inches behind the ball, blasting it out in a spray of sand, water or long grass. Your follow-through should be low to the ground with your hands and the handle remaining ahead of the club-head. The ball will pop up and have a lot of roll once it hits the ground.

You can experiment with loft of the clubface when practicing this shot. By opening the face of the club slightly, you may be able to get a little more loft from some buried or obscured lies, but never forget that the only real goal is to get the ball back in play.

The Driver Off the Deck

One of the most useful trouble shots I've come across utilizes the longest and hardest-to-hit club in your bag—your driver. I've known touring professionals and other talented players who hit the driver off the fairway for distance, but for most golfers, I'd recommend using the driver from the ground in a much different manner.

With its relative lack of loft and the natural low, left-to-right shot that the driver will produce, it's a great way to get a powerful fade that flies close to the ground and under-neath any overhanging trouble. With the roll you'll get when the ball hits the ground, this shot can advance you anywhere from 170 yards or more, making it very valu-

The driver can be a secret weapon when you've got to keep the ball low but still want to hit it far.

able on long par-4s and par-5s on which you may have driven into trouble.

Rather than playing this shot like a traditional fairway wood, you'll want to play it more like a knockdown iron shot. In other words, grip down two to three inches on the club's handle and move the ball back slightly in your stance. Resist the temptation to maximize the loft of the clubface by playing it up in your stance—the goal here is to hit a hard line drive. Use a firm grip pressure in both hands to resist the release of the club at impact.

Line up left of the target, with the clubface aimed at the point where you'd like the ball to start. It should curve 15–20 yards to the right.

Make your regular length backswing, using the hands, arms and shoulders to control the length and pace. Your lower body should remain quiet, the hips turning minimally in response to the rotation of your upper body.

Keep your normal swing pace for both the backswing and forward swing, and trust the club to do most of the work. Try to clip the grass as you let your body rotate through the shot while keeping your hands, arms and club in a low finish position.

THE UNPLAYABLE LIE

Although this chapter should help you escape from many of the less desirable situations you find on the golf course, there will be some times when you simply cannot make a swing at the ball, or, even if you can, you'll have nowhere to hit it. In these situations, your only alternative is to take an unplayable lie.

The penalty for an unplayable lie is one stroke, but that may be a far more appealing alternative than spending four shots trying to hack your way out of thick underbrush. When you take relief from an unplayable lie, you have three options for putting the ball back in play.

The first option is to take a drop within two clublengths of where the ball has come to rest. The problem is that this option often doesn't provide complete relief from the obstacles. Even if it does, you may not have a clear line back to safety.

The second option—and one that many golfers overlook—is to go back as far as you like, keeping the spot where your ball came to rest between you and the hole. Greg Norman used this option brilliantly in the 1997 Bell South Atlanta Classic. In contention on the final day, Norman severely hooked his tee shot at the par-4 17th hole. He located the ball, but had no way of advancing it. Even with a two clublength cushion, he couldn't make clean contact. So he retreated. He ended up dropping the ball about 75 yards behind its original position. From there he could clear the trees and was able to put his next shot on the green. Remember, a longer shot can sometimes be an easier one.

The third option is to return to the spot from which you played the previous shot. This is the least attractive of your three options because it is, in effect, a stroke-and-distance penalty.

Knowing your options when faced with an unplayable lie can minimize the damage. And that's what getting out of trouble is all about.

Chapter Summary

THE STOP-AND-GO

Setup

- Use at least one more club and possibly two (e.g., if the distance calls for a 6-iron, use a 5-iron or even a 4-iron for this shot)

- Grip down one to two inches—or far enough to avoid the tree limbs above you

- Ball position one inch back, with hands slightly ahead of the ball

Swing

- Swing back to your stopping point, placing the club in proper position

- Hold your top-of-the-swing position for a full one-one thousand count

- Begin the forward swing by dropping your hands, arms and golf club to the ball

- Rotate your body fully to the target

- Low finish

Strategy

- Know your capabilities—can you pull the shot off more than half the time?

- Weigh risks vs. rewards: consider an unplayable lie vs. risking disaster and a big number or possibly hurting yourself

- Take a number of practice swings to find the proper stopping point short of your obstacle

- Shot will come out low and will run more than normal

- To get the timing of this shot, make sure you practice it on the range before you use it on the course

Swing Thoughts

- Smooth tempo on the forward swing is key—try not to generate too much clubhead speed at the start of the forward swing

- Low finish

Practice Strategies
RESTRICTED SHOTS

There are plenty of times when you find yourself under a tree or up against a fence and are forced to execute a shot with a restricted swing. Sometimes taking an unplayable lie and a stroke is the best course of action, but if you know how to tackle a shot that restricts your swing you don't always have to resort to a penalty stroke.

Drill

The stop-and-go drill is one I sometimes use for players who need to learn to hit the ball from the proper top-of-the-swing position. Start by placing a ball on a tee at the range. With a middle iron, turn your upper body away from the ball and swing the club to the top of the backswing and stop. Feel the club in a balanced position at the top of the swing. Then swing the club down, letting it build speed gradually and resisting the temptation to jump at the ball. Remember, you're going to use this shot as a recovery from trouble, so the key here is solid contact, not power and distance.

The trick to pulling off the shot during a match is having experienced the shot, or at least a very similar one, in practice. Take a minute at the end of your practice sessions to give yourself a challenge. Your task is to create a nearly impossible situation and think your way through it. Remember, your goal is to advance the ball and avert disaster. Your practice will help you learn what your limitations are in difficult situations. You want to find your comfort level and build your arsenal of recovery skills. Challenge a friend to a tough shot—which one of you can get out of it in the best shape?

Index